SANTIAGO'S GUITAR

Book Two of the Reluctant Pilgrim series

STEPHEN R. MARRIOTT

Santiago's Guitar
By Stephen R. Marriott
www.stephenrmarriott.com

Paperback ISBN: 978-1-912615-92-6

This book is written generally using
British spelling and grammar.

To my dad, Roger Marriott

Contents

PART II

They are not long, the days of wine and roses:
Out of a misty dream
Our path emerges for a while, then closes
Within a dream.

- Ernest Dowson,
from *Vitae Summa Brevis*

Prologue

Papá,

Not long after I'd completed my pilgrimage to Santiago, an amigo remarked that I was no different a person to the man I was before I left our village. Well, he was wrong. The old Diego would never have been crazy enough to return your guitar to your ghost in Sarria. Let alone walk to the edge of Spain and write this note in the sand to his deceased father!

And if I had returned home for good, everyone in the village would eventually have seen me as they'd always done because for them everything was still the same. But here I am watching the waves washing onto the beach like sea-weary pilgrims and listening to the seagulls cry, "Ay de mi." I would never have made it this far if you had not gifted me music and a stubborn resolve to keep walking.

I have lived a life on this walk, and some unbelievable things have happened on the way. And one day, when I join you in that house in the sky, I'll tell you this story of my Camino.

Gracias,
Diego

Part I

1
Just a Long Walk

It was the thought of a cold beer that had kept him walking. Diego had shaken off the last remnants of the fever that had left him bedridden during his previous days in Sarria, but again his body ached. He stretched out his legs and rested them on the opposite chair under the table. His walking fitness had gone now, and Santiago was still some 100km away, which he had learned from two pilgrims as they'd climbed the hill into Portomarín.

The waitress delivered his *caña* and he removed his Stetson from his head. He reached for the small glass of draught beer and drank it in one long glug. More pilgrims hard-footed it by while passers-by snuck into the shade of the Medieval church before Diego, and he began to suppose, was it not just a long walk he was on, nothing more? Would his life really be any different at the end of it? He whispered, "This is *loco* in July!" *Wouldn't it be nice to spend the rest of the day under the shade of the stone arcade with a cerveza and see which señoritas crossed the plaza and came out to play once the sun dropped?* he thought. Then he scolded himself for thinking that way; he shouldn't allow his weaknesses to get the better of him and delay his journey.

The church bells began to chime and, for the first time in the day, he felt a waft of air on his cheeks. He looked up at the church, its parapets decorated like battlements, and then as his eyes traced back down to the street they followed locals and pilgrims entering the building for Mass. He had the idea that it might be the coolest place in town. It was still too hot to march around looking for a bed for the night.

He paid for his beer, shouldered his backpack and stepped towards the building. Then he remembered he'd left his empty guitar case propped against the table. He collected it and went into the church.

Diego sat at the back, rested his eyes and his head dropped forward as the rhythmic words of praying rocked him to sleep. When it ended, he jolted back, and he wasn't sure if it was the change of tone in the church that had awoken him, or something else, but he found his eyes drawn up to the curves of the vaults leading down to the chiselled faces of noble-looking men. After the Mass, Diego headed over to one near the altar and stared up at it to take a better look. Noticing Diego's interest in the effigy, the father stopped beside Diego on his way to the vestry.

"*Un Caballero de la Orden de Santiago*," the father said, removing his glasses and arching his back up at the face. He dropped his voice to nearly a whisper, "They're all members of an ancient order, similar to the Knights Templar, sworn to protect the medieval pilgrims on their way to Santiago."

Diego jumped with surprise, as he hadn't noticed the priest arriving beside him. He regained his composure and replied, "Important men then?"

The father replaced his glasses. "*Sí*. Whatever age we're in, the Camino has always found a way to help the pilgrims on their journey." He gripped his bible and papers firmly and said, "*Buen camino*," thereafter he continued to a side door.

Diego glanced again at the other Knights before he discovered himself lighting two candles, one each, for his mother and father. After he collected his backpack and case, he left the church with the objective of finding a bed for the night.

~

RECORDINGS OF GREGORIAN chants echoing around the hostel slowly roused Diego. He'd fallen into a deep sleep almost immediately after arriving at the nun-managed hostel and resting his head on his pillow. As he dressed, the music gilded his body like the first rays of sun painting the fields. And as he wandered into the dining hall he thought of his desire; it was clear and untainted, though still far away. He sat at a long table across from a nun, who was still humming the music.

"A nice way to start the day," Diego said, reaching for the coffee pot.

The nun stopped humming and looked up.

"It's how I reconnect to God each day," she said softly.

The nun held herself demurely and Diego couldn't tell if she was old or not.

"I've been coming here every summer for as long as I can remember," she continued. "Madrid is too hot this time of year and no one thinks of church, so I come here to volunteer. It's my way of giving back to the Camino."

"Giving back to the Camino?"

"I once walked it, when I was looking for some answers. And it led me to my church in Madrid."

Diego realised he was still holding onto the coffee jug and he gestured across to the nun and she smiled. Diego filled her cup and his own, then asked, "The church is a lifelong commitment. You ever regret it?"

"There were times early on when I wondered if I was doing the right thing, forfeiting a husband and children. But faith takes time and as it took root I understood you have a duty to fulfil your divine purpose. I don't need anything more, because in serving the church, I have it all. God made me understand that…"

"Hmm. It seems like He asks for a lot of sacrifices."

"Define your idea of God."

"I'm sorry I respect your opinions, but I can't answer that; it's not something I think about."

"God is a different concept to different people but the unifying thing He teaches us is love, and love is passion for who you are."

Diego took a sip of coffee and momentarily closed his eyes. He had not fully woken up and was in no mood for being preached to. "I've never been one for deep conversation at the breakfast table; do you mind if we change the subject? How far is it to the next town?"

The nun put her coffee cup down, leaned across the table and met Diego's eyes. "God leans on those who are determined to have what they really want. Do you not see anything in the church?"

"Let's put it this way, I'm starting to respect the people who uphold the values of the church, like *Los Caballeros de Santiago*," replied Diego with widening eyes.

"Then you appreciate faith. They will help you with your walk."

"Who?"

"People are passionate about so many things, their smartphones, music, Netflix and everybody loves food," she said passing Diego a bread roll from a basket. "But they've forgotten about the one thing they should be really passionate about, living their true lives."

Diego broke the roll in half and dipped one piece into a dish of tomato pulp and chewed over the nun's words. He took a sip of coffee and sighed, "That's a lot to think about this early in the morning."

The nun smiled. "I can show you a shortcut."

∽

DIEGO ADJUSTED HIS hat to protect his face from the sun rising over the pine trees. He batted away a fly, and wondered if he was going a little mad as he paced along the dirt road detour. The nun's idea of a shortcut, via the resting place of the Knights of Santiago, had already added a kilometre and he figured he'd have to walk back the same way. But he kept walking and eventually, from behind more pine trees, three stone arches revealed themselves. They beckoned Diego through them and towards the church's iron door. It was unlocked, so Diego slowly opened it.

The air inside was damp. When his eyes adjusted a little to the dark, he rested his baggage against the side of a pew towards the back and sat down. He closed his eyes and thought he could hear water dripping. A minute later he reopened his eyes and fully took in the church's interior.

Over his right shoulder there was a chalk-coloured stone effigy of a prominent knight lying on top of a stone coffin with elaborate engravings. Mould spread like a green canvas on the wall behind it, making it look like the knight was sleeping in a field. Glancing further around, he saw more effigies of knights; some sat upright, resting against headstones, and there were more coffins with knights lying on top of them as if they were asleep. He got up and approached a stone canopy protecting the Virgin and to its side were candles, tempting him to light two. As he lit them, the flickering light revealed other things: under his feet, the flagstones were engraved with simple crosses, and scallop-shell carvings dotted the walls. And a decaying fresco was of Christ in a paradise abounding with fruit.

A drop of water landed on Diego's neck and a cold shudder ran through his spine. Suddenly, he felt the need to leave. He retreated to the back, grabbed his things and left the building. The sunlight blinded him and he sought refuge on a bench partly protected by the broken shadows of the arches. He screwed his eyes tight shut and fell asleep.

The smell of onions wafted by Diego's nose and a hand tapped his shoulder. His eyes opened to sunrays glistening amber on chainmail armour. He blinked a couple of times and the knight sitting beside him removed his helmet. His curly dark beard, grey around the chin, and sharp eyes seemed as real as he'd seen on any man.

"Ah, that's better; damn hot in there. Do you have a smoke?" asked the knight. "Thought I had a pack on me; can't seem to remember a thing these days," he continued as his words merged into a booming laughter. "Guess I'm getting old!"

"Am I dreaming?"

"I don't know. You might have been. Sorry to wake you, but I always like to get here first and get into character. It'll be a while before the others arrive and I'm gasping. You do smoke?"

"Err yes, roll-ups," replied Diego with a confused tone.

"Ah, a man who appreciates tobacco."

"Just got into it recently; better value for money, I've found. But what are you doing here?" Diego figured that, if he was dreaming, he might as well play along with it.

The knight smiled. "Why I am a *Caballero de Santiago*." Then he pointed to a cross, fashioned as a sword painted on the front of his mantle. "Do you not recognise our mark?"

"I wasn't totally sure," replied Diego as he reached into a pocket for his tobacco tin. "But I guess you are! Are you going to give me a lift to Santiago on your horse?" He looked up from the cigarette he was making. "Having said that, I can't see your horse…"

The knight's beard shook with laughter. "Sorry to disappoint – that's not really on the agenda today. I'm part of a re-enactment society; we're putting on a display later."

"I thought so," said Diego, feigning a grin. "Just helping you get into character."

Diego hurriedly returned to making the cigarette, trying to hide his embarrassment. He lit it and handed it to the knight. "Enjoy."

"Thank you, pilgrim," said the knight, before taking a long pleasurable drag.

Diego began rolling his own. When he was finished, he looked up and asked, "You called me pilgrim. How did you know?"

"You enquired about a lift to Santiago, and there's also your pack," said the man glancing at Diego's backpack. "During our re-enactments, I spot the odd walker like yourself coming up here on their own. Some might call you dreamers, but I wouldn't."

"What do you mean?" said Diego, lighting his own cigarette, then taking a drag.

"You're prepared to embrace the unknown as you seek out your passions. Most people have forgotten how to live with uncertainty; they can't even leave the house without checking the weather on their smartphones. The truth is you don't know what's at the end of your road, but you walk anyway. That is a true pilgrimage. But you also have the humility to ask for help. That's why you seek out the Knights. The very fact they take vows of obedience to serve the pilgrims, to serve their purpose, is the strength of character you wanted to feel. Can I share a story with you?"

Diego nodded.

"Turn out your pockets to a stranger and one day you will win the lottery."

Diego eyed him curiously and the knight flicked ash from his cigarette before he continued talking.

"La Orden de Santiago was formed to protect the pilgrims from attacks by the Moors. Pilgrims would often gather in the fields around here, waiting to be escorted to Santiago on the last leg of their journey. One day, the Knights were informed of a large battalion of Moors riding north towards the pilgrim path. The Knights rode south to confront them; it was a close and bloody fight on a high ridge and hundreds were slaughtered, but the Knights came out the victors. After they buried their own dead, the Knights mounted their horses and were ready to leave the scattered bodies of their foes to rot. But one Knight, the knight I play in the act, shouted after his comrades and reminded them they should also honour their enemy in death. The Knights saw reason and dismounted.

"For another day they toiled in the hard ground without food or water. And after burying their fallen enemies, they blessed the ground. Some years later, my knight received at his door a cartful of grapevines from a sultan in the south, who lived near a great river close to the border with what is now Portugal. One of those Moors, who'd been buried on that hill, had been the son of the sultan. For years the sultan had been searching for the man who'd initiated the burials, wanting to repay that man for giving his son an honourable burial. Thereafter, the knight never went without wine. Legend says it is the knight buried in there." He nodded towards the church. "The one lying on the ornate coffin."

"Really!" said Diego.

The man smiled and turned and looked under the arches. "No sign of the others? It's too hot to be sitting out here waiting for them; I'll take a quick nap inside," he said, gesturing at the church again.

The knight stood up, collected his helmet from the bench and stubbed out the butt of his cigarette. "That was a fine cigarette. *Buen camino*, pilgrim."

"*Gracias*," replied Diego.

The man turned and rested a hand on the grip of his sword before disappearing into the church.

Diego noticed a strand of red ribbon on the bench where the knight had been sitting. He picked it up and thought about going into the church to give it back to him, but then a sudden gust of wind blew the ribbon up and towards the tops of the pines, and they arched, as if pointing westwards. Diego shouldered the backpack and lifted his guitar case.

Walking back down the path, Diego noticed red butterflies with black dots on the hems of their wings dancing between the hedgerows; sometimes they would skirt within whiskers of each other, but they never became entangled, finding their own flight paths again. When he reached the end of the path, Diego spotted a yellow Camino arrow painted on a stonewall pointing right. He stopped, took a drink of water from his hip flask and glanced up at the burning sun. "They say too much *sol* makes you *loco*," he said laughing aloud. Diego wasn't sure if he'd just met a real man or the ghost of a knight. He put the flask away and tightened the straps on his backpack. Next, he turned to follow the arrow and continued on his way.

2

Crossing the River

As Santiago loomed, Diego stopped at each church in the many rural villages he passed through to light his candles. Most of the time, he was the only visitor, apart from a cleaner dusting, or sometimes a widow praying at the front. But in one church, just as he was leaving, men carrying a coffin above their heads emerged through the door, shadowed by a procession of mourners. Emotions welled up inside him and he felt compelled to stay.

He sat on the edge of a pew and began crying, imagining the service Padre Jacob would have given for his father, but he mainly cried because of a memory he had long stopped having until it had returned in that moment. Papá and he were sitting on sticky leather seats in the back of a black car and the round shoulders of the driver and the undertaker framed the image ahead: the rear of a hearse displaying its content like a tapas cabinet. That content was his mamá's coffin. When his tears stopped, he shivered and left the church.

THE REMAINING FEW days blurred into long country lanes, occasionally broken up by dilapidating farmsteads worked by stocky farmers and their wives droving cattle from the sheds and into the fields. The afternoon breezes brought the waft of eucalyptus and comfort to Diego; reminding him of an ointment his mother had once rubbed on his chest when he was very young and had a cold. The eucalyptus also had the effect of thinning the omnipresent smell of manure and damp foliage.

During one of the days it drizzled throughout, but he felt warm in his denim shirt, and his Stetson kept the rain off. He smiled contently, remembering how his friends had made fun of him whenever he wore that hat. And in the late afternoon, when the drizzle petered out and the sun broke through the clouds, the flowers flourished. Carnations, roses, marigolds and hydrangeas glowed brightly in the hedgerows. A nearby tractor engine hummed, and the birds began to chatter, like old men gathering in a local square to gossip after an afternoon *siesta*.

Although Diego's guitar case was now empty, music was never far away. On his penultimate day, while crossing a medieval bridge, pipe music floated up from the river. He looked over the bridge and saw a man sitting cross-legged on the river's edge, blowing meditatively on a wooden flute. The music blended with the gurgle of the water, and it brought to mind the endless summers he had spent beside the rivers and tributaries with his *amigos*. He reminisced over how the water cut around the knees of the fly fishers and the fascination he and his young friends experienced looking into their keep nets at the strong but imprisoned trout. And he remembered the watermarks on his trousers from catching grasshoppers in the long wet grass that they sold for bait to the fishermen.

Later they would feel like kings as they walked into Bar Paradiso, with money in their pockets to buy colas.

There they debated the flamenco legends, and who might knock the great guitarist Paco de Lucía off his perch. Ricardo would argue for Tomatito, firmly believing he was the purest of the guitarists, contending Paco de Lucía had strayed too far away from flamenco's gypsy roots. Though Diego would have none of it, arguing that this was in fact Paco's strength. Javier didn't care much for music, and would sway the conversation to football, a subject where their opinions changed like the wind, depending on the new signings of the big clubs. Diego had been right though; throughout Paco de Lucía's life there had been no one to match him. Other than his father's playing, Paco's music was the first he'd heard, and Lucía was the reason he'd grown his hair so long.

He wondered why his papá had got rid of his old vinyl records. They'd be worth a fortune now. But he knew the answer to that question; he'd always known the unmentionable – why his father had been unhappy. Diego kicked a stone and pushed on, trying his best not to think about the past.

3

Santiago

Diego awoke early in a woodland cloaked in morning mist on the edge of Santiago. He didn't dwell; breakfast only consisted of two squashed cereal bars, a swig of water and a cigarette.

An hour later he arrived in the city's suburbs; the Gregorian chants from the nun-run hostel looping in his head as he reached the medieval centre. Waymarks in the cobbled streets led him to the main square, Praza do Obradoiro, and he rested his luggage in its centre, dropping his hat onto the pile. He ran his hands through his hair and felt alone; he was one of a few people in the vast plaza. Though he saw some pilgrims in their sleeping bags around its edges, presumably having walked through the night.

He cast his eyes around looking for a café, and as he did, he noticed there was a trickle of pilgrims arriving, usually in a pair or a small group. One dropped to his knees and made the sign of the cross, and others took photos with the stone-weathered grey and yellow cathedral as their backdrop. Diego stared up at the cathedral's ornate steeples and wondered how many commitments to change the cathedral must have heard whispered below its bells over the centuries.

It was a moment he wanted to share, and he reached into a pocket for his phone, forgetting he'd lost it in Bar Paradiso the night before he'd set out on his pilgrimage.

Then, under a medieval arcade, he spotted someone who looked familiar, rolling up a sleeping bag. His beard now hid more of his face, but he thought he recognised the stocky man.

Diego cupped his hands around his mouth and hazarded a greeting into the thin light. "*Buenos días*, Basque man!"

The man surveyed the plaza, and when he spotted Diego, he saluted him with, "*Chico!*" And then he strode towards him.

"I see you're still sleeping in strange places, Leonardo!"

The friends grinned at each other before Leonardo pulled Diego into a bear hug.

Leonardo released his grip and, looking Diego over, ventured, "How do you feel, Diego?"

"Good but weird at the same time. Does that make much sense?"

"*Amigo*, it makes perfect sense." Leonardo's eyes gleamed like polished chestnuts in the early light. "This is when your Camino really begins."

A bell of the cathedral chimed. As they listened to it ring six times more, Diego contemplated Leonardo's words. Though he had known his life would no longer be the same when he reached Santiago, he'd avoided making plans; as long as he was walking, it didn't seem to matter. But now it was time. Reunited with an earlier companion from his walk who'd given him the prod he needed to continue, he was again here with his no-nonsense advice. Diego breathed in deeply as plans and ideas gurgled up through his body. He smiled and said, "Coffee?"

They collected their belongings, left the plaza and took a seat outside a nearby café opposite the Pilgrim's Office;

where a handful of pilgrims had gathered patiently outside its locked door to receive their *Compostellas*. The official certificate awarded for completing the Camino. Leonardo offered his friend a cigarette and they smoked contentedly.

"Remember Juan?" Leonardo said after blowing some smoke through his nostrils.

"How could I forget him? He secretly put some money in my pocket. Thanks to that man I had my best night's sleep on the Camino."

"He's a prince. He did his best to impart to me all his knowledge of the trees and natural world along the Camino. I stayed at his place for two weeks, and now I feel I know even less about horticulture! Funny, I thought the Camino would lead me miles from home, now it's taking me back. I will register all the existing trees in the forests around my village and replant the cleared forests with native trees to help restore balance to the natural environment."

"That's wonderful."

"*Sí.*"

"My Papá died recently," whispered Diego as he removed his hat. "I heard a few weeks ago when I was in Sarria."

Leonardo leaned across the table towards Diego.

"He had me late in life and was very old. But I never gave him the respect he deserved as a father. And I never learned his stories or treated him seriously. I thought at times he'd given up on me, not just himself. You see my mother died when I was very young."

"He sounds like he was a good man."

"He was troubled but, in the end, I think he made his peace. He was watching out for me on the road and I saw him when I played at our campfire. Did you see him?"

Leonardo half-smiled and shook his head.

A waiter delivered two large plates of ham and eggs, a basket of pastries, coffee in a French press and orange juice.

"Did you order all this?" asked Diego.

Leonardo grinned. "Let's call it a present from Juan for making it this far."

Diego smiled, stubbed out his cigarette and got stuck into the food.

Leonardo leaned across the table and retrieved a bottle of rum from under his fleece and added some rum to the coffee. He grinned and said, "A little twist of Basque."

As they ate, Leonardo noticed the line of pilgrims steadily growing outside the office and mentioned he'd like to get his *Compostella*. Diego hadn't picked up a pilgrim passport en route, and so hadn't had an official document that could be stamped at the bars and *albergues* as evidence of walking the Camino. But he didn't mind, and although Leonardo's document with all its stamps looked like a possession to treasure, he knew in himself he'd walked the Camino and that was enough. After all, it had given him a much bigger reward; the courage to pursue his guitar dreams. So after their breakfast, they went about their own tasks but arranged to meet at noon for the pilgrim's Mass.

The waiter had told Diego about a guitar shop just outside the old town. On the way, he playfully stepped over slivers of sunlight striping the narrow Medieval alleyways. He stopped for a moment and peered through the window of a restaurant displaying local produce, including an octopus. Its curled tentacles and red suckers appeared alien against the hunks of meat and shellfish, like a Baroque still life painting. It wasn't long before he found the shop. It was closed, so he sat down on the front step and smoked a cigarette, observing people emerging from apartment blocks and darting into their cars. The arrival of the shop assistant then broke his thoughts.

"Hey, you have to move on. I need to open up," said the man with an American accent but in Spanish.

Diego looked up and replied, "I'm here to buy a guitar."

"Ah, okay, *bueno*." The man gestured at Diego's Stetson. "Cowboy, I can give you a good deal on a Gibson, only one owner. It plays like a dream."

Diego smiled, stood up and stubbed out his smoke. "I'm a flamenco guitarist," he said, following the man into the shop.

It didn't take Diego long to make a decision because the shop mainly sold electric guitars and only had a small range of classical guitars, and even fewer flamenco ones within his budget. It wasn't perfect but his chosen guitar felt dependable; it's back and sides felt solid enough in his hands and it was the same colour as his father's, though deprived of the darker blemishes of maturity. Its spruce top gave it a raw and alive flamenco sound and it reminded him of a working man's wine, earned with toil and sweat during those long harvest seasons. That's how he saw his new guitar, which was paid for by those evening performances outside *Federico's* in Sarria. And it would continue that way. He would perform in the *peñas*, and other flamenco establishments until he was plucked out of obscurity, and had gone as far as he could go with that guitar.

Outside the shop, Diego threaded his arms through the straps of his backpack, placed the guitar inside the old case and held it in his right hand. And as he wandered back to the cathedral, the case swung evenly from his right arm, like he was holding a briefcase. On the way, he noticed Santiago's buskers forming around the old town; a number had the look of drifters and alcoholics and he'd wondered how long they had been there and whether they would ever leave.

He queued with the other pilgrims outside the cathedral, and was glad that cloud masked most of the sky above the plaza. He would take any shade he could get. Though it was cooler in Santiago, the mid-July sun was still a big test of his resolve. The line moved quickly, and before he knew it, he was entering through the large wooden doors.

A rope filtered them towards the nave and a sign, stating luggage was prohibited. Diego looked down the line of people and he could see he was the only one with his backpack. He was thinking about how he might slip by with his gear when a female steward approached him. Diego instinctively smiled broadly at the middle-aged woman and, without thinking, he began recounting in detail his morning spent buying his new guitar and how he hadn't had time to drop his things anywhere, adding with artistic flair that his previous guitar, an antique, had mysteriously disappeared on the Camino. It had been like losing a brother, he told her, and there was no way he could leave his new guitar unattended; it would break his heart to lose another brother so quickly. The woman smiled curiously and ushered Diego through.

The cathedral swelled with pilgrims, but Diego found Leonardo sitting at the back with space beside him. He winked at Diego, then bent his head forward and began to pray. Diego removed his backpack and sat down. Placing it and his guitar in-between his legs. He craned his neck around looking for Isa, although he didn't really expect to see her sitting amongst the congregation, as she would have completed her Camino some weeks before. She had been the reason he had kept walking on those first days on the Camino, and he wished he could now thank her, and come clean about what had been in his head.

He glanced back at Leonardo, who was still praying; a man he'd met in the clearing of a forest, someone that found peace as soon as he'd set off on his pilgrimage. Was he really the father he wanted? But Diego told himself no, that's not who Leonardo had been to him. The older brother he'd never had? *Perhaps*, he thought. Then it came to Diego; the reason you don't get to choose your parents like you do your friends is because your parents need you more than you need them. In his case, he needed to complete his papá's work, to reach flamenco's greatest heights. Then a great sadness fell over Diego as he figured this would be his last meeting with Leonardo.

Loudspeakers announced that photography was forbidden during the service and the noise dropped. Priests in white robes and sashes, with the emblem of the Santiago cross, gathered around the altar, and tears trickled down the faces of many of the pilgrims. Diego also wanted to cry, but he wanted to cry alone and he couldn't endure a drawn-out parting with Leonardo after the mass had finished. And after all it was Leonardo who'd stated that his Camino was only just beginning. It was time to take action. He patted Leonardo softly on the back, stood up and slid one arm through a strap of his backpack. Leonardo looked up and smiled and reached out a hand. Diego took hold of it and, to his surprise, it felt smooth, like the exposed layer of bark on a tree. They shook hands and Diego stepped away from the pew and forced a smile through his sadness. He waved goodbye with a small sweep of his hat, and as he left, he asked a steward to point him in the direction of the bus station.

4

Passing Through

Diego peered through the window of Bar Paradiso. It was dark and a glass refrigerator lit just one corner of the bar. He removed his gaze from the window and took a few steps away from the bar's terrace towards the village plaza. His eyes adjusted to the dark and he surveyed the square; the silhouette of the church of San Pedro was as still as the night, and the only sign of life was a dog sniffing around shop shutters on the far side. Momentarily, he closed his eyes. When he reopened them, he looked down and noticed beside his feet a metal plaque on the site of his father's old candyfloss pitch, the light from the moon trimming its edges silver. He knelt down and placed a finger on it and read the inscription:

Eduardo García Sánchez, Guitarrista

Beloved Husband and Father.

Diego ran his fingers along the engraving, and looked up at the moon before it disappeared behind the clouds. He stood up, stepped back onto the bar's terrace and reached a hand into the pot of a palm tree plant. From underneath the bar's neon sign, he tossed a handful of soil at the first-floor window. A curtain flicked and a heavy-eyed Arnau peered around it and down at the figure bathed in incandescent turquoise.

"Diego?" whispered Arnau, opening the window.

"*Sí*, it's me," whispered Diego. "Let me in. I'm starving."

Wrapped in a dressing gown, Arnau ran down the stairs, unlatched the main door and pushed aside the beaded curtain. Diego picked up his belongings and followed Arnau through the bar and up the stairs to his apartment and into the kitchen. Arnau's questions began as soon as he grabbed a couple of eggs and cracked them into a frying pan. At the top of his mind had been Diego's whereabouts the night of their phone call, the night he told Diego that his father had died. As Arnau sliced a baguette, Diego explained a little sheepishly that he had been close to finishing his Camino, not quite knowing what Arnau would think about his decision not to return immediately.

Arnau flipped the eggs onto a plate, added some cured ham and placed the food on the table. "*Claro*, for sure you needed to complete your pilgrimage, but you kept me busy those weeks you were away. Mind you, we sent your Papá off in grand style. I've taken care of most things but there's still some papers waiting for you to sign. In the morning, I'll call Martín's office. Now eat."

Diego dropped his packs in a corner of the compact kitchen and sat at the table. He removed his hat and said, "Catalan. Papá and I owe you a drink."

Arnau washed his hands in the sink, and ran a hand through the thin strands of his hair. "Well, his passing is definitely bad for business – his candyfloss cart was always a good excuse for parents to take a seat at the bar," said Arnau, grabbing two bottles of *Alhambra* beer from the fridge. "But for now let's drink to him. Tomorrow you can find out if Eduardo stuffed away a fortune, then maybe you can buy me a drink." He sat next to Diego, took a sip of his beer and nodded over to a mobile phone on a corner of the work surface, "Your phone's over there."

~

WORD OF DIEGO'S return had spread around the village, which turned his short stroll to the lawyer's office and back into a pilgrimage in itself. Though the village had long been associated with the Camino, villagers went out of their way to greet Diego and ask about his experience as well as offer their condolences. It seemed to him a little strange they treated him like a celebrity. He knew any of them were capable of walking to Santiago. It wasn't so far. They just had to believe they could.

When he returned to Bar Paradiso, Ricardo and Javier were waiting for him. He was happy to see his old friends, and thought they could hide away in a corner of the bar undisturbed.

"So are the drinks on you?" joked Ricardo as he got up from their usual table and hugged Diego.

"Tell me about the *mujeres* jóvenes on the Camino," retorted Javier with a wink as he stood up and greeted his friend.

"Let's get a table inside," said Diego, gesturing towards the door, "And I'll tell you about the women in there."

Javier nodded at the table. "But this is our usual spot. We didn't once give up your seat while you were away."

"You didn't have to do that, but if you don't mind, I'd prefer a little discreetness this morning."

Javier eyed Diego a little suspiciously before pulling out a plastic chair. "Let everyone see you're back, besides it's too hot inside. You know Catalan; he's too tight to turn on the air-con before the afternoon!"

Diego glanced at Ricardo, who responded with a shrug of his shoulders. Diego sighed inwardly but sat on the chair. Javier patted him on the back, then he nipped into the bar.

"You're okay?" asked Ricardo.

"I'm sad, of course, but Papá was very old and everything had been taken care of thanks to Catalan. I'm lucky it all worked out so simply."

"Arnau's a good man."

"*Sí*, he is. He's always looked out for Papá and me."

Javier returned gripping three *cañas* and placed the beers in front of them. They clinked their glasses together and Diego took a sip, leaned back into his chair and stared across the plaza. People were going about their business under a pale blue sky, occasionally blemished by thin wafts of clouds screening the midday sun. Among a group of walkers, a female pilgrim, with a backpack high on her shoulders, strolled through his vision and he was reminded of his liaison with Isa, a month before on the steps of the very same church. The chance conversation with the Dutch *chica* had changed everything. His friends could never fully understand the significance unless they themselves walked the path to Santiago. He thought how simple it would be to hit the trail again. Walk, eat, sleep. And occasionally play the guitar. *Wasn't that enough?* he pondered.

"You don't feel any different?" asked Ricardo.

"*Qué?*" responded Diego.

"Has it changed you?"

Diego looked away from the plaza and across the table at Ricardo. "Maybe. Time will tell."

"You're still the same old Diego," said Javier, saluting him with his glass.

"I'd like to walk it someday," said Ricardo.

"You will, when the time's right for you," suggested Diego, nodding at the church and the route of the Camino.

"We should have done it all together. What made you take off like that, Diego?" interjected Javier.

"It's best walked alone. Right, Diego?" said Ricardo.

"Well, you're back now," said Javier. "You can speak to Catalan and put on that gig you were talking about. Remember? We can help spread the word."

"And you can crash at my place until your money comes through," added Ricardo. "My parents insist."

The conversation was distracted by the arrival of Arnau, collecting their empty glasses and swiping at a fly. Arnau gestured a glass at them and Ricardo responded, "Add it to my tab."

"There's not much money left, what with the funeral and Martín's fees!" said Diego.

Arnau glanced at Diego with curious eyes. Diego responded with a reassuring tip of his hat, suggesting everything had been settled to his satisfaction at the lawyer's office. Arnau disappeared into the bar.

"*Padre* Jacob claimed the church found the funds for the funeral?" quizzed Ricardo.

"Come on, you really think Eduardo would have allowed anyone to have paid for him. He had savings."

"You could sell candyfloss," said Javier.

Diego adjusted his hat. "Amigo, I'm leaving later today. I'm going to ask Arnau to sell the candyfloss cart and anything else I don't need."

"You've always looked ridiculous in that hat," stammered Javier. "But now you're making no sense at all!"

"But where will you go?" asked Ricardo.

"I'm going to become a *Madrileño* cat and move to the city, performing in the flamenco *peñas* and *tablaos*," declared Diego.

"They're not your people in Madrid," said Javier defiantly. "You won't crack that coconut. Be realistic, Diego."

"You're the one who put the idea in my head; you're always talking about your cousin living there. Can you give me her number? Perhaps she knows somewhere I can stay."

"We'll come with you," responded Javier, glancing towards Ricardo for support.

"I'm sorry, but this is a one-man show," said Diego, leaning forward. "Ricardo, thank your parents for their kind offer, but I won't be staying."

"But you belong here; it's where you're from," appealed Javier.

"Just phone your cousin," said Ricardo as he gestured to Arnau through the window of the bar for their beers. "One for the road then!"

"Always," said Diego with a smile.

The long shadows of two headstones stretched across to blue and pink bursts of hydrangea climbing the walls of the cemetery. Diego knelt and placed two burning candles by the graves. He stood and took a couple of steps towards a small gate at the far side of the cemetery, before briefly stopping and glancing back over his shoulder at the resting places of his mother and father.

He continued to the gate as Arnau's old Peugeot pulled up. Arnau leaned across the passenger seat to open the car door. Diego got in and they sat in silence as Arnau drove. The route to the train station had once seemed very familiar, but the more they drove the less Diego recognised the winding road.

Arnau drove them into an empty car park outside the local station. He got out of the car, leaned against the bonnet of the Peugeot and lit himself a cigarette. Momentarily, Diego stayed in the car contemplating whether he was doing the right thing. But he got out boldly and Arnau passed him his backpack and guitar case from the rear of the car.

"Do you want me to wait with you on the platform?"

"It's okay. They'll be bashing your door down if you don't get back to the bar soon."

Arnau wanted to ask Diego to reconsider his decision, but he saw, standing in front of him, a man ready to choose his own roads. Instead, he kissed Diego on both cheeks and said, "Remember, we'll always be here anytime you feel like returning."

"I appreciate everything you've always done for me, and especially for Papá during those afternoons he'd had too much to drink."

"Someone had to look out for you Garcías. Just repay me by playing something uplifting at my funeral. None of that depressing stuff."

"Get away with you," said Diego as he put his arms through the shoulder straps of his backpack. "You'll outlive us all."

He felt the weight of the pack on his shoulder and adjusted the straps. Then he picked up his guitar. Diego reached out his spare hand and in Arnau's firm grip he felt a man grounded to his place in the world. They let go, and Diego went into the station and bought his ticket.

He waited alone on the platform and watched the minute hand slowly click its way around an old wall clock. The train finally lugged into the station, and an austere-faced train guard got off and pointed him along the platform to his carriage. Diego pulled himself onto the train and stood at the window, trying to pinpoint how he felt at that moment. But he couldn't describe his feelings. All he felt were the vibrations of the train as he watched the station disappear, and the dipping sun paint the sky tangerine.

5

El Barrio

Diego shared his carriage with two young men, who didn't say much and were connected to their laptops through their headphones for most of the journey. He took the top bunk on one side of the carriage and, for the first time in his life, he felt completely alone. He was no longer a pilgrim walking the road to Santiago. No longer the son of the local candyfloss man. *Even tramps gather together with a sense of belonging*, he pondered. He shuddered and felt the icy breeze of the train's air-conditioning. But, at that moment, in that cocooned space, in that flicker of panic and despair, the boy from the village was gone. More than ever, he was Diego the flamenco guitarist. He felt the vibrations of the train and its wheels taking him steadily south and furthering him from his old life.

He reached for his guitar case at the end of the bed, puffed a pillow behind his head and removed the guitar. Then he went about tuning it.

DIEGO WEAVED IN and out of the commuters as he made his way from the train, along the station's concourse and into Madrid's streets. He was desperate for a smoke and found a space next to a newspaper stand and bought some roll-up papers. Diego found comfort in the vendor's, "*Buen día*", the everyday greeting of good morning, and felt part of the city's daily mass movement. He made his cigarette and, as he smoked, he reflected on his panorama. The modern cathedrals of the day, glass skyscrapers glinted in the sun, rising above a bridged highway and into a pastel blue ocean of sky. And from a nearby subway, a saxophone diluted the hum of the city.

"All you have to do is play," said Diego. "Play with imagination, play like you believe it and they will give generously." He realised he was talking to himself, and wondered how long he'd been doing it. Then he figured it must have started on the Camino, during those long spells he'd been walking alone, and he made a mental note to stop, especially in public, before it became a habit and people thought him *loco*. He reached into a pocket, pulled out a napkin and looked down at the address and telephone number scribbled in black biro between the creases. When he looked up he noticed two policemen standing further down the street, observing people entering the station. He stubbed out his cigarette on the paving stones, gripped the handle of his guitar case and strolled over to the officers.

"*Buen día*," said Diego.

One officer removed his sunglasses and eyed Diego's guitar case and the other folded his arms.

"Is this street far?" continued Diego, showing the squinting officer the napkin.

"Just arrived in Madrid?"

"*Sí señor*,"

"Planning on staying a while?"

"That's the plan."

"Show me your ID card," said the policeman brusquely.

Diego removed his wallet from a pocket, retrieved his ID card and bit his tongue.

The officer glanced at the card and passed it to his colleague. The other officer unfolded his arms, removed his sunglasses and took a closer look at Diego and inspected the card. He then nodded and handed the ID card back to the first officer.

The officer snapped the card into Diego's hand and nodded in the direction of the subway, "You can take the Metro, ask them there."

"*Gracias!*" said Diego, though he had wanted to mock them with, " *¡Bravo, bravo!*"

The smell of hash blending with curry spices met Diego at the street level. He took one step away from the Metro exit, dropped his gear and took it all in. He was in a neighbourhood plaza, in the centre of Madrid, but he could have been anywhere.

Parasols were popping up outside a row of Indian restaurants. Two buskers outside a 24-hour supermarket were setting up an improvised stage consisting of a small amp and an open guitar case, in which they placed CDs. Hanging from railings around a playground in the centre, he noticed an artist selling pictures featuring street scenes. Children scrambled around the playground and Arab-looking mothers exchanged the latest gossip from a nearby bench. Elderly Spanish men sat at a bar terrace drinking and browsing through newspapers. And across the plaza, a group of African men with sharp eyes, occupied one corner. He drank it all in, then picked up his things and walked across the plaza to look at the names of the narrow streets snaking up a hill.

Diego skirted past the gang of Africans.

"*María?*" whispered one of the gang from behind bright yellow sunglasses.

"Marijuana's not really my thing. I'm looking for a street, perhaps you know it?" Diego pulled out the napkin and held it out to them.

One of the Africans, a man in his mid-twenties, was sitting at the step of a shuttered shop covered in graffiti. He combed his Mohican hairstyle, then stuck his comb in his wiry hair and came over. He was tall and wore a basketball vest. "I can show you," he said in Spanish but with a throaty-sounding French lilt. The youthful African reached out a hand towards the napkin. "Most streets familiar to me around this *barrio*."

Diego handed him the napkin.

"I know it."

An older looking man nodded at Diego, his braided dreadlocks brushing his phone. "Nothing else to do in this heat than be indoors and smoke. Sure you don't want a little marijuana?"

Diego shook his head.

The youthful African gestured towards Diego's guitar case. "Let me help you with your guitar case."

Diego strengthened his grip on the handle, pulling it in and responded, "*Gracias* but I can manage it"

The African placed his comb in a trouser pocket. He smiled broadly and said as he swaggered off, "Come on, it's not far."

Something in his boyish smile made Diego trust him, and he followed the African out of the plaza and up a narrow street. They exchanged names as they cut up the hill and Diego learned he was called Mamadou.

"*Hace mucho calor*, no?" said Diego as he felt the sweat dripping off his forehead.

"Too hot in the summer, too cold in the winter in Madrid, brother."

Diego glanced at a general store and replied, "Think they might sell a cold *cerveza* in there?"

Mamadou stopped. "Probably but it's too early for me. I prefer to take a drink at the end of a day, when my work is done. But go ahead."

Diego was thirsty, but he didn't fancy drinking alone. "You're right. Best I find my accommodation."

Mamadou continued walking and Diego followed.

"Want to know the oldest advice in the book?" asked Mamadou.

"Go on?"

"Temptation, brother. It's in the Qur'an and your Bible and yet most people don't heed its warning."

Diego cocked his head towards Mamadou as he walked beside him.

"Nothing wrong with a man drinking a beer or smoking a little *maría* but, in a city like this, there are many temptations. When the going gets tough, as it always does, it's easy to give in. But drinking too much and fooling around is the quickest way to kill your dreams. I learned through my brothers here in this *barrio*; they showed me the way when I was down on my luck. The only way forward is to get pleasure in your daily labour, share your skills and love your neighbour. It's a philosophy we Senegalese live by."

Diego eyed Mamadou curiously.

"Work helps me hold onto my dream. I arrived in Spain with just my sabar drum strapped to my back, wide-eyed and dreaming of the drumming school I'd build one day. I was working as a fisherman in Dakar and, when I got my chance, I paid smugglers and they took me to Morocco. From there I sailed in a small fishing boat to Spain. We were picked up by the coastguard and taken to Almería, but because I was young then, I was not detained and I found work nearby and did whatever I could to survive. Later, I heard about an opportunity to work on a construction crew in Madrid, so here I am.

"African brothers show me how to fill in visa forms and get residency. It was good times; they were building many tenements in Madrid and I saved money, and every day I felt I was a step closer to my dream. Then one day, like a tsunami, the financial crisis came and swept away our jobs and my sabar school. I took jobs here and there, but when there was no work, I had to check out of my hostel and leave my things at friends' places. During those times I drank too much, I did stupid things, you know. But the more I drank, the more I gave into temptations and the more I felt hopeless. Sometimes I would make any excuse to stay late in a bar and drink myself sorry, even when I had money for a hostel. Eventually, I forgot why I had come to Spain and my spark went out.

"One day, I got into a fight with a Senegalese brother over a bottle of beer. But I got lucky because another brother, from Senegal, broke it up. That man we call Picasso, you met him earlier, the older man; he took me in with other brothers. Ours is a house of painters, carpenters, artists and musicians. But in harder times, when there is less work for our talents, there are always things to trade in the streets and subways: bags, umbrellas, Spanish fans, shoes, whatever will sell. Every sale I make, I think of as another brick of my school. To be a man, to be yourself, you have to work hard, and it will make you strong and you think less of temptations.

Like it says in the Bible, all will be well when you eat the fruits of your labour."

Diego pondered his words as they reached the top of the hill and turned right into a wider street lined on both sides by tall apartment buildings.

"Brother, it doesn't mean I never sin," said Mamadou with a laugh. "Just be careful. It's ruined many an artist."

Mamadou's cautioning brought to mind Paco de Lucía's former sidekick, the famous singer Cameron de la Isla. Paco went from strength to strength but Cameron died penniless because of his addictions. *But Paco was lucky*, Diego thought. *He'd had a Papá who'd drilled him in the guitar twelve hours a day and not a father who preferred having a drink and made broken promises. But I can do it. Just have a couple; a reward when I've earned good money.*

"What makes you think I'm an artist?"

"A fellow artist always recognises another," Mamadou grinned. "Besides, you have a tight grip on your guitar; you must be serious about your music."

"Guess so, I've got a plan you might say."

"Me too. I will return to Africa when I have the money for my music school."

Mamadou stopped outside a cream apartment building.

"This is it?" inquired Diego, looking up at the building's ornate balconies.

"*Sí señor*, welcome to *el barrio*." Mamadou reached out his fist and Diego brushed his knuckles with his own.

Mamadou turned to leave and removed his comb from his pocket. But glanced back over his shoulder and said, "You ever need anything, I'm always around." Then he began walking back down the street.

"*Gracias*," yelled Diego after him.

Diego checked the napkin and then pressed a buzzer. The shutters to one of the higher balconies flew open and a young woman with auburn hair stepped onto the balcony.

"Diego?" she hollered down.

"*Sí, buen día*," shouted Diego, looking up.

"It's nearly afternoon now. I'm Letizia. I'll be right down."

She slammed the shutters behind her and, moments later, opened the door. "Come in and I'll show you what's what," she said, reaching out a hand. Diego smiled, shook her hand and followed her into a dark hallway and tried his best to keep up as she darted up five flights of stairs and into the apartment.

She led Diego into a small kitchen-diner, consisting of a round wooden table with a single chair at the kitchen end, and at the other was a sofa next to the shutters leading to the balcony. Opposite the sofa was a cabinet, with both its doors hanging open revealing a television.

"We're going away for the rest of the summer to Cadiz."

"You're going on holiday?"

"*Sí*, it was a last-minute thing; my boyfriend managed to negotiate more holiday with his company." Letizia pointed to keys on the table. "The place is yours until the end of the summer, if you like. And if you leave before I'm back, just lock the door behind you and drop the keys in the post box in the hallway." She then turned away from the table and stepped towards a door and gestured for Diego to follow.

Javier had kept quiet about his cousin's beauty, he thought, as Letizia opened the bathroom door and pointed to the shower next to an open window looking out over red rooftops and the south of the city. Next, she opened a door opposite the bathroom, leading into the bedroom. A double bed took up most of the room, and on its mattress was a suitcase. Pointing towards the bed was a pedestal fan.

"There are clean sheets in the bottom of there," said Letizia, gesturing to a simple but antique wardrobe, "and you can hang your clothes on that rail," she continued, pointing at a rack of woman's clothes the other side of the bed.

Diego put his case in a corner and glanced at her. She met his eyes and said, "I remember you from school."

"Really?"

"I was in your art class."

"You were?" Diego grinned broadly. "But I would have remembered you."

"I had braces and looked different then, it was quite a few years ago."

The beeping of a car horn from below in the street interrupted the conversation.

"I told him I'd be on time for once; he hates it when I'm late." Letizia grinned as she grabbed the suitcase off the bed and stepped towards the door. "He's German, you see. You were always drawing pictures of lonesome men with guitars. Well, I can't keep him waiting. Call me if there's any problem – you have my number. Enjoy, the place is yours."

"*Sí. Gracias*," stammered Diego after Letizia. As she dashed out of the apartment, the main door slammed behind her, knocking a framed Picasso print against the exposed living room brickwork.

Diego dropped his backpack and hat in another corner and thought how unfortunate and lucky he'd just been. "You're going?" he said aloud, thinking he'd liked to have got to know this cute *chica*. But it was also a result getting the place all to himself. He opened the wardrobe; under a rail of clothes were bed linen and towels and Diego reached for some sheets, but as soon as they were in his hands he found himself returning them and opening his backpack and pulling out his sleeping bag. He spread it across the bed and then went into the bathroom. The world was still as he urinated into the toilet and stared across the rooftops and distant brown hills. When he finished he washed his hands and went back to the bedroom.

Diego sat on the end of the bed, pulled off his boots and switched on the fan. He fell back onto the bed and, before long, the whirring tones of the fan had sent him into a deep sleep.

6
Inori

A shop shutter rattling somewhere in the street below woke Diego. He reached for his phone on the bedside table and looked at the time; it was two minutes past five in the afternoon. He sat up and twisted his body to catch the breeze from the revolving fan and slid onto the edge of the bed. For a few minutes, he sat, like a bird perched on an isolated cliff, gathering its strength and thoughts, before he stood up and went into the lounge. He opened the shutters, stepped onto the balcony and gazed across at the rooftops and neighbouring balconies.

He viewed a couple of people shortening the canopies protecting their balconies from the sun and wondered who they were and what they did. And he thought of Paco, and what his first view of Madrid would have been. He'd once read that Paco's father had moved the whole family from the south of Spain to Madrid, just to foster Paco's music career. And he'd been very protective of his son's talents, holding him back from the *tablaos,* and there was the legendary story of one flamenco club paying ten times the going rate for Paco to perform. Diego looked down into the neighbourhood and wondered where the nearest *peña* or *tablao* might be. He supposed he'd accept a tenth of the going rate, just to get a foot in the door.

He felt his shirt sticking to his back, and he thought about taking a shower. He left the balcony, threw off his clothes, collected a towel from the wardrobe, grabbed his washbag and went into the bathroom and took a shower. He felt the weariness of the road in his bones as he turned the water to cold. He stepped out of the shower feeling refreshed, and dried off the condensation that had formed on the bathroom mirror with his towel. With his hand, he felt the black whiskers of his small beard and figured it had been at least a week since he'd last shaved. Diego took out his razor and shaved. When he was finished, he felt his smooth face with his palms.

He dressed, collected the keys off the table and headed to the front door. But as he placed his hand on the door handle, he stopped, about turned and went back into the bedroom. He reached for his Stetson, rested it on his head and strode into the bathroom. Glancing into the mirror, he adjusted the hat so that it sat at a slight angle on his head. Then he left the apartment.

Diego retraced his steps back along the street, turning down the hill. He took a closer look at his new surroundings, noticing the mixture of cultures. Some shop signs were in Arabic, and general stores offered products and food from all around the world: Bangladesh, India and Africa. The buildings were uniform, but occasionally broken up by individual large doors, some were metal and studded and others were made of heavy wood, containing panels twisted into motifs of wheat bushels and scythes. He also spotted that some residents didn't care much for banks; one ATM had been covered in graffiti.

The smell of marijuana wafted in his direction. He followed the aroma and it led him off the street to the steps leading down to a new plaza. Behind him he spotted a 'hole-in-the-wall' shop. The plaza below had a ruined basilica on one side, and evening drinkers were dotted along the other three sides. At the foot of the steps, Diego spied Mamadou with his comb lodged in his hair and sitting with some of the gang of Africans from earlier.

He glanced back up at the shop, with a cold beer on his mind. Momentarily, the idea was tempered by Mamadou's earlier cautionary words, but buying some *cervezas* for the gang would make a nice introduction, and it was Friday night, after all, he thought. He also figured the remainder of his money would last at least a week, now he had the luxury of no rent. Diego strolled over to it and ordered eight cans of beer and a packet of mixed nuts from a Chinese man. The vendor put the items into a plastic bag and Diego headed down the steps into the plaza. Picasso caught site of Diego's shadow and looked up and said in Spanish, "Another white man wanting to be a Rasta." The group roared with laughter and feeling a little foolish Diego held up the plastic bag and said, "*Cerveza?*"

Mamadou reached out a hand and said, "Ignore him, brother."

Diego smiled and handed Mamadou a can, then passed out the beers to the others. Mamadou patted a spot on the step next to himself and Diego took a seat and cracked a beer open. They all chinked beers and Diego was grateful for their company. Though it wasn't long before they went back to talking amongst themselves in their native tongue. Diego opened the bag of nuts and ate a handful and Mamadou tapped Diego on the shoulder and said, "Hungry, brother?"

"I'm permanently hungry these days," replied Diego, offering Mamadou a handful of the snack. "Ever since I started out on the Camino de Santiago trail. You know it?"

"Of course. I may be from Senegal, but I've lived in Spain long enough to learn some of your customs. You come here after you walked to Santiago, I guess?" Mamadou flicked a nut in the air and tilted his neck back to catch it.

Diego took a swig from his can and a long shadow from the neck of a guitar suddenly appeared, tapered on the steps below him. Then a man holding a guitar greeted the gang with their ubiquitous hand gestures. He was wearing a white linen shirt and had long sideburns running down from under a straw trilby-style hat. He was youthful and Spanish. Mamadou introduced Daniel to Diego and, after they exchanged their names, Diego asked, "Daniel, you've been playing for long?"

"Too long," offered Daniel. "Should have given it up a long time ago!"

"Why do you say that?"

"It gave me romantic ideas and distracted me from what I should have been doing."

"And what's that?"

"Carpentry is what I'm good at, but I once kidded myself I could make it as a Spanish guitarist. I love the guitar, but it seems it's the crafting of wood that people prefer to pay me for."

"You play in the streets though?"

"*Sí*, just for fun or occasionally for a little *cerveza* money – there's not much work around for carpenters at the moment. You play?"

"Yes, the flamenco guitar. That's why I'm here in Madrid."

"Gutsy, *amigo*,"

"*Loco*, more like," said Diego with a smile as he offered Daniel a beer.

"It's not crazy if you have good reason," replied Daniel as he received the beer and cracked it open. "Why do you like the guitar so much?"

Diego reached for the final can in the bag, opened it and momentarily thought about the question as he drank. "No one's really asked me that before," and he put the can down. "My father put a guitar in my hands when I was very young and ever since I've always played. Well, on and off. Guess you might say it's a kind of escape. It senses my mood and listens without judgement, and understands me in the way that nobody else can. Does that sound weird?"

"*Inori*," said Daniel.

"*Inori*? You mean to have *duende*?"

"No, *duende* is that raucous moment of passion between the artist and their fans. *Inori* is more personal. It's your prayer – it's a Japanese word. A spiritual idea. It's faith in who you are and a life without prejudice. That's what I think you might be saying. When you play, you draw on the great power we all have inside ourselves and it gives you faith. When you're in that state, you have the purest belief that your prayers will be answered."

Diego had been listening to Daniel with his head bowed and, as he contemplated his words, he tilted his head back up and looked about the plaza. Everything still looked the same, but now everything seemed slightly different after Daniel had spoken. The guitar had always been telling him there was more out there, beyond the fields and rivers of his village, and now this idea of *Inori* had emerged. *But why had the guitar never done the same for Papá. Why had it not renewed his faith after Mamá's passing? But Papá eventually had faith in me, and I will repay that*, he thought.

Diego turned his attention back to Daniel and said, "Carpentry is your *inori*?"

"*Sí*, it helps me when I'm having a bad day, or it helps me learn when I'm having a good day as well. When my chisel slides through a piece of wood with grace and love I ask myself, 'Why is it so easy today when yesterday it was so hard?' And then I am one step closer to understanding myself."

"You said *inori* is a Japanese word?"

"I did. An ex-*novia* of mine was Japanese. It's how she explained what flamenco is to the great flamenco performers."

"She's a dancer?"

"She tried; like you, it's what drew her to Madrid. She wanted to learn at the best schools. But although she danced well enough, the standards are very high and, while the teachers were very kind to her, you will never be truly accepted into that world unless you have flamenco in your blood. And eventually she came to understand that and she left."

"Where is she now?"

"She went back to Tokyo, where I believe she's now making a living as an interior designer."

"I'm sorry it didn't work out for her, and I'm sorry your relationship didn't work either."

"That's okay. We had a good time, and we learnt a lot from each other. We're both survivors."

Diego felt the need to play and thought about going back to the apartment to fetch his guitar. But the beer was already making him feel sluggish and, instead, he asked Daniel, "May I play your guitar?"

"Of course," replied Daniel, handing his guitar to Diego. "But it's a classic guitar, not flamenco designed."

"They're all from the same family," said Diego enthusiastically. He rested the guitar on his leg and played a chord. Then he plucked some more notes, before he twisted his playing hand and quickly brushed the strings of the guitar and it began to bob lightly up and down on his leg. He closed his eyes and adjusted his chin, almost resting it on the curved side of the guitar. He remembered Papá saying, "Take a deep breath, draw the guitar in close and think about how you feel today. That will be your *palo*, the style you will play."

As he started to play, Mamadou and the Africans gathered around Diego. Suddenly his fingers raced across the guitar frets and he began to sing. His voice was loud and throaty, drawing people from the plaza. The light faded fast and his denim shirt blended into the backdrop of night. The glow from a street lamp caught the guitar. Diego's torso was just a blur against the sheen of the wood and his lightning-fast fingers.

He became more playful and improvised a gypsy rumba and a song:

I saw the sea in the stars,
By a river I did rest
Then a boat sailed my way.
Salida its name, my payday.

A caged lion shared my deck,
He stopped me jumpin' thrice,

Wet and hungry, our gods gone,
Roars, 'Is darkest before dawn.'

It was a full moon that night,
When Almería caught our sight.
One day we'll return by plane,
And wave adiós to Spain.

I labour with the guitar,
But not for wine and roses,
It's my craft, the lion in my heart…

He didn't know how long he'd been playing when he heard what sounded like the tumbling rhythm of surf interweaving with his music. Opening his eyes, he saw a wooden drum between Mamadou's knees, its base resting on a couple of steps below. He played the drum with one hand and a stick in the other, and Diego noticed carvings of birds and a lizard on the drum's base. Mamadou nodded to Diego, gesturing for him to continue, and as Diego did, some of the younger members of the crowd danced playfully, making up their own versions of flamenco and African dancing.

When their performance came to an end, Mamadou chinked Diego's knuckle with a knowing clenched fist, then he reached for the joint that had been doing the rounds and passed it to Diego. He took a long puff and blew a smoke ring into the air and handed Daniel back his guitar.

"*Gracias,*" said Diego.

"No, thank you for reminding me I should always stick to carpentry. I have never heard such brilliant music played on my guitar before."

Diego passed the joint over to Daniel, and he took a quick drag before he passed it onto one of the Africans, a man with arm muscles the size of watermelons.

Diego glanced back at Daniel. "How well do you know the flamenco scene here in Madrid?"

"A little, though it was my Japanese *novia* who had the contacts. But I can take you to a bar where flamenco people sometimes hang out after a show. Perhaps you'll make a friend there. But I'd start at the schools; audition, or just perform for one of the teachers. Someone there will surely recognise your talent and be able to help."

"But what about in the *tabernas* or bars that host gigs?"

"There's always an opportunity at those places for good musicians, but earning sensible money, that's the problem."

"Will you show me that flamenco bar tonight?"

"Sure, but it's a bit early yet."

"*Claro.*"

As the beer flowed, the conversation on the steps reverted to football and *señoritas*. Occasionally Daniel played some melodies and by the time he suggested they should leave for the flamenco bar, Diego was in high spirits and ready to experience some more of Madrid. He turned to Mamadou and said, "You'll join us at this bar?"

"Not tonight, maestro. I need my sleep, Saturdays are our best day in the streets," he replied adding a wink. "Treat those *señoritas* well."

"I'll be gentle with them," said Diego with a grin as he dusted Mamadou's knuckles with a clenched fist. "See you around?"

"Definitely, brother."

They said goodbye to the gang and Daniel led Diego up the steps, out of the plaza and into the night.

They each bought themselves a can of beer from a man on the street and as they walked towards the centre, Diego tried to take the city in. It was intoxicating and a far cry from his Friday nights at Bar Paradiso. He tried to visualise himself sitting on the terrace but he couldn't see himself there. In his mind's eye, he just saw Ricardo and Javier drinking and joking. It was home and had been a way of life. But as he cast his eyes around Madrid's shadows, peppered with bright street lamps he realised he'd been blinkered in his village. They passed lively tapas bars; statues; theatres; dark cobblestone alleys and homeless people asleep in the doorways of historical buildings, and before Diego knew it, he was descending steps to a drinking den and striding over to the bar.

Scattered across its walls were photographs of the flamenco greats; Paco was there in one corner, and Diego felt him staring expectantly at him with bulbous eyes. Behind the bar was the large landlord, a man with grey hair mopped over a ruddy, round face that sank into his shoulders. Two men stood at one end of the counter looking up at a flat screen television and a flamenco video.

"*Señor*," Diego said with authority, "two red wines." He glanced at Daniel standing beside him and added, "You like red wine?"

"Of course."

"*Bueno*, it feels like a place to drink wine."

"*Ribera* or *Rioja*?" replied the landlord.

"*Ribera*," responded Daniel.

The landlord served them the wines in shallow beaker style glasses and Diego raised his glass to Daniel and said:

"¡Gracias!"

"For what, *amigo*?"

"Friendship."

Daniel chinked Diego's glass. "Welcome to Madrid, Diego."

Diego smiled and took a glug from his glass. Then a group in fiesta mood burst through the door and into the bar, shortly followed by two men and a young woman, who instantly caught Diego's attention. The men were dressed in black, one was lanky and the other had a goatee beard and was carrying a guitar, and the woman was wearing a white, cotton summer dress, vivid against her long dark hair and exposed skin. A fringe partially covered one side of her face. They took a table in a dim corner.

"Do you know them?" asked Diego, cocking his head in the direction of their table.

"No, but I've seen them in here before. They perform at one of the *tablaos*."

"They have that look of performers," said Diego, gathering his thoughts, thinking of a way to introduce himself. "And what about her? She's beautiful."

"A dancer, I believe."

"I've got to meet her."

Daniel grinned and raised his glass to Diego. "I like your style. What are you waiting for?"

"Err, the right words."

"You'll think of something, maestro."

Just then the man with the guitar placed it on his lap and worked his fingers down the frets, played a chord and struck the soundboard of the instrument to add percussion. The music was primitive, and yet it demanded Diego's attention. The guitarist's companions relaxed back in their seats and the melody continued simply but there was a fresh crispness to every note. Diego glanced at Daniel, who nodded back at him knowingly. The guitarist had an edge that Diego couldn't rightly explain. His music was intimidating but also inspiring.

Diego knocked back his wine and ordered another one as he gazed on with awe. After a couple of songs, the guitarist put his instrument down and the lanky man got up and approached the counter. Diego reached for his glass and took another glug, then glanced at Daniel. "Pass me your guitar."

Daniel handed it over to Diego with a smile. And with his spare hand, Diego readjusted his hat. *Here we go, say your prayers*, he thought. Daniel watched on as Diego walked over to the table with a slight wobble in his step, gripping tightly on the neck of the guitar. When he reached the table he said, "*Perdón*, you perform at one of the city's *tablaos*?"

"*Sí?*" replied the guitarist, rubbing a finger across his goatee.

The other man returned, placing their drinks on the table and the woman immediately took a sip from her glass of sherry, as if to avoid replying to Diego. The man sat down, took a drink of beer and folded his arms.

"You're an amazing guitarist," continued Diego.

Both men looked blankly back at Diego.

"Err, apologies for the interruption," muttered Diego. "We haven't met before. But my name is Diego and I'm looking for work as a flamenco guitarist, preferably at a *tablao* and I was wondering if you knew anywhere looking for someone?"

The two men smirked at each other in reaction to the audacity of Diego's question. And after a moment the guitarist said, "You can't just walk into a *tablao* and expect to get hired. I've trained for years and bided my time. Unless you're of exceptional talent the reality is that it could be years before you might get a chance to play at a decent *tablao*."

Diego shrugged his shoulders.

The woman flicked her fringe and found herself saying, "Maybe he is talented." She looked up at Diego. "Are you going to stand there all night or are you going to play something?"

Momentarily, Diego was speechless, entranced by her vulnerability, which she sheltered with her sharp tongue.

"*Señor?*" she said.

Diego distracted his gaze from her brown eyes. "Sure, I'll play something." He pulled the guitar into his chest and instinctively twisted his strumming hand and it brushed up and down the strings with a rumba. Diego upped the tempo, forcing them to bear witness to his strumming agility but the strings jerked awkwardly as Diego's shaky hand missed a couple of them. He banged hard on the guitar's soundboard and swayed a little. Then he pressed his fingers weightily on the frets. A string snapped, and the music stopped, like a horse suddenly becoming lame from being pushed too hard by its rider.

Diego coughed and said, "Guess the classical guitar isn't built for a rumba."

"No guitar is built for that kind of zealousness," said the lanky man.

The woman flicked her hair and looked away.

"*Amigos* I can play you something else. I can fetch my own guitar, or maybe I can borrow yours?" pleaded Diego.

Daniel stepped over and placed a hand on Diego's shoulder. "Let it be," he said taking back his guitar. "I think you're all played out for the night."

"Ugh, okay, sorry about the string."

"It's just a string," replied Daniel as he led Diego away to the bar.

From the counter, Diego stared across to the table but the flamenco artists had already gone back to their own conversations. Diego glanced back at Daniel, "One for the road?"

"You're not done drinking?"

"It's the weekend; I intend to get drunk."

"Okay!"

Diego leaned across the bar, grabbing the landlord's attention with a simple, "*Otra*."

The man looked up from the leg of cured ham he was carving and obliged by grabbing a wine bottle and topping up their glasses.

7

Hotel California

All morning, Diego had been sitting at the table outside the café eyeing the students going through the doors of the glass-fronted indoor food market across the street and ascending the spiral steel stairway inside to the flamenco school, on the top floor. He had the feeling of a non-commissioned painter who could never present their paintings to a gallery in case they had to explain it, in case they got found out, in case an aficionado remarked, 'You're not a real artist!' Now his hand was unsteady after drinking three *café solos*, black coffees.

JUST BEFORE DIEGO had stumbled out of the flamenco bar on the Friday night, Daniel had scribbled the name of the school his Japanese girlfriend had attended on a napkin. And all weekend he'd argued with himself about going. But he always came back to thinking that Daniel spoke much sense and he should check it out.

He hadn't seen much of the weekend, spending the afternoons on the sofa watching Spanish football on the TV, and a number of times he'd considered texting Ricardo and Javier about the unfolding scores in the pre-season games, and entering into their usual mockery based on their teams' results. Diego was a *Barça* fan, Barcelona, it was also Arnau's team. Every time

Barcelona was on TV, Arnau would show the games in the bar. And seeing Arnau's face when Barcelona won a game had enticed Diego in from an early age. But Diego abstained from contacting his friends; knowing the quick fix of text banter with his *amigos* would not relieve his hangover or make him feel any happier. Instead, he'd toughed it out on his own, rejecting the lure of going out in the evening; knowing he needed to give himself a fighting chance on Monday when he'd begin his search for paid work as a guitarist.

DIEGO HADN'T EXPECTED to feel so nervous. But all he could think about was being exposed by the people in the building he was now facing. But the reality of Monday was here, and it was time to commit to his dreams. He told himself just one more cigarette and then he would cross the street and climb the stairs to the school. Diego made the cigarette and took small drags on it. But he still finished it too quickly for his liking. There was nothing else to do but to go across to the school. He stood up but a rattling metallic sound from behind distracted him. And he glanced over his left shoulder and spied a man padlocking up the shutters to a fishmonger's shop. Painted over its shutters was a mural splashed in pink with images of fishermen pulling a skiff from a foamy sea, the waves breaking onto the shore, towards other small fishing vessels nestling in the sand. A jagged rock on the beach, mimicked the shape of a camel sitting on folded legs looking out to the horizon and seagulls dotted the panorama. Diego looked at his phone, it was just after two, and he noticed people leaving the school.

Siesta time, he thought. *I'll come back later*. But really he knew he wouldn't be returning.

He dropped his head and turned down the first street that led away from the flamenco school. He despised himself. His *amigos* had always seen him as someone who was bold, but he knew that was a lie. It was only true when it came to approaching women or confronting someone in a bar who might have spoken out of turn. He'd walked to Santiago and yet he couldn't face the few steps that would have taken him into the school. What would the people in his village think? He stopped for a moment and glimpsed through a shop window displaying female flamenco shoes and thought about other opportunities he'd wasted and promises he'd made.

There had been the time he'd got his first job through a family acquaintance; a trainee clerk in the office of a local tractor dealership. In the days leading up to that job, he had told himself and Papá that he would work hard and learn everything there is to know, and one day perhaps he'd open his own dealership. But he only lasted one morning. Leases, finance, warranty, certified pre-ownership; all the jargon and administration had overwhelmed him; and at lunchtime, when the office emptied, he jumped through the back window and ran into town and took the part-time job at Bar Paradiso that Arnau had said was always waiting for him. And when he'd worked the grape picking seasons; after a hard day's labour and with a glass of wine in hand, he'd often stated to his fellow pickers he would go learn about wine production at college. However, the idea of college scared the hell out of him; he hadn't even completed high school.

Diego passed by more flamenco outfitters and the street opened into a pedestrianised area, with an almond tree, surrounded by a low brick wall. He rested on the wall seeking to escape the sun and himself. He bowed his head and said aloud, "Will you man up, Diego?" A couple of minutes passed and he reached for his wallet. He already knew he'd spent most of his cash during Friday night's extravagance in the bar with Daniel; nonetheless, he opened the wallet. All that was left was a ten Euro bill and a card from the late night flamenco bar, *Copas Anton*. He looked at his bankcard, again thinking he would be wasting his time in trying it but miracles could happen. He slowly stood up, took hold of his guitar case and looked about for a bank. There were none in sight, so he continued along the promenade until it brought him to a commercial street and he spotted a bank across from him. He waited at a pedestrian junction for the green man and crossed over to the bank and put his card in the ATM. He pushed the button to check his balance. There was just €4.33. Diego ejected the card and put it away in his wallet.

It was a strange feeling having no money again, during his time busking, having a full wallet had fuelled his belief and reassured him he was on the right track. *Be a man*, he thought. He removed his phone from a pocket and typed *tableu* into its mapping app. It threw up a number of them and, as it turned out, one was just a few blocks along the street.

In less than five minutes, Diego was standing outside a frosted glass door. The club's neon sign wasn't lit, but he could still make out its name: *Arte del Flamenco*. He took a deep breath and tried the door. To his surprise it opened, revealing a narrow corridor with a reception desk leading to another door. There was no one there, and so he crept in. He slowly opened the second door and he observed a stage with a flamenco dancer, contorting her body into the shape of a crescent moon. She wore a leotard and a ruffled skirt over black leggings and, to Diego, she looked more like a ballerina than a flamenco dancer. A man with pronounced angular features, a chiselled jawline, long tangled hair, and skin like a hardy leather belt was instructing her. He was dressed all in black, apart from a long mauve scarf garishly hanging from around his neck. Only the stage was lit, and Diego slid unnoticed through the door and sat in the dark at a table towards the back.

Diego counted the dancer repositioning herself into the same pose fourteen times before her choreographer was satisfied. Then she began a sequence starting with that pose before she extended her right arm high and bent her other arm at the elbow and turned her hand in and rested it on her thighbone. She closed her eyes and arched her neck back. Next, she stuck out her right shoe, and raised her heel, so her weight rested on the ball of her foot. The choreographer stood back and sat at a table beside the stage, all his attention focused on the performance to come.

The heels of her rosewood shoes echoed around the room and her shadow danced on the wall behind her. Occasionally, she cupped clapping hands as she ended a sequence. The pulsating sound reminded Diego of a ticking school clock, but sped up to a musical rhythm. The choreographer encouraged her with an occasional, "*Olé, olé*, Andalucía" and Diego began to comprehend further the significance of *inori*. *When you say a prayer it can be anywhere*, he thought. And they might have been in a school classroom for the lack of the dancer's awareness of her surroundings at that moment. When the performance ended, the woman stepped down from the stage and sat with the man at the table as she reached for a bottle of water and Diego approached them.

"*Bravo, bravo,*" he said. "*Gracias*, it was a privilege to experience that."

The dancer looked up in surprise and the choreographer said, "Who let you in?"

"Err," replied Diego as he scanned his mind for the right answer. "Apologies I didn't mean to intrude, but the door was open, and I want to meet the best flamenco artists in the city."

The woman took a sip from the bottle and the choreographer regarded Diego with narrowing eyes and said, "Well now you can tell your friends you've met us. But we have much work to do."

"*Sí*, I'm lucky," said Diego, wondering who he was actually talking to. "But can you spare a minute or two, I'm a guitarist," he gestured at his case, "and looking for work. Can I play you something?"

The man responded by resting a thumb under his chin and rubbing it with his index finger. The dancer got to her feet and went back to the stage.

"People pay a lot of money to come here and we've got a big performance to prepare for tonight," said the choreographer, standing up. "This isn't the right time for an audition. You know many people come to Madrid trying to make it in flamenco. Play where you can, make some *amigos* and if you're any good they'll tell you. Then come knocking on my door. Save us both some time."

Diego thought upon his words and simply replied, "*Gracias*."

The man nodded at Diego and joined the dancer on the stage again. Diego headed for the door, but he glanced over his shoulder before he left. He caught the dancer in a static moment, outstretched, like the limbs of a tree, and he saw in her images of himself playing his guitar along silent roads.

He left the building and stepped across to the street's west side and into the shadows of tenement blocks to avoid the sun. He wondered who he'd just met, and cursed himself for knowing the names of football players, but not the names of the famous flamenco artists. He pulled out his phone, looked at the mapping app and stubbornness drove him onto the next nearest *tableu*. But he found its door locked and Diego said aloud, "¡*Madre mia!* What doors should I knock on Paco? Or better still, ask your Papá please." He glanced around for inspiration but suddenly felt very hungry and strayed down the street on the lookout for a cheap restaurant. On the way, he passed a barman unloading crates of bottled beer from the back of a van beside a *taberna*, and clinking of the bottles prompted Diego to casually ask about work and if the place hosted music. The man told him to ask inside, and to Diego's surprise, the boss said '*Sí*' to both questions. They were booked out with regular performers, but an opportunity to perform on their modest-sized stage might occasionally come up at short notice. And a barman on site who played the guitar would be in a good position to jump in he told him. Diego didn't immediately put himself forward but took a card and continued along the street and came across a little pizza café.

He bought two slices of pizza and a *caña* and received four euros fifty as change from his ten euros. The food and beer were as good as any he'd ever tasted and he ate and drank cautiously, not sure where his next meal would come from. After he'd eaten he took a closer look at the card he'd just pocketed. The *taberna* was called *Casa Cerveza*, and the card stated in smaller lettering: *international beers and music bar*. Diego was tempted to go back and take the job, but he hadn't come all this way to be a barman again. He wanted things to be different, to earn a living from his music and not be waiting around to take the stage. Instead, he got up and pushed on along the street, and towards the city's historical centre.

He arrived at a large cobbled plaza, lined by rows of peach-coloured apartments, terraced with countless small balconies, built over an elegant arcade that ran along the perimeter of the plaza. Under the shade of the arcade were many restaurants. Diego walked into the middle of the plaza to take in its full majesty. On the way, he looked around and noticed a street sign: Plaza Mayor.

The mid-afternoon sun was strong and he pulled the brim of his Stetson over his forehead. The restaurants were busy, and scattered around the edges of the square the odd street vendors displayed their wares, in the shade of the apartments. A man dressed as a bullfighter, selling polka dot flamenco dresses, looked hopefully towards the restaurants and posed with an occasional tourist for a photo. Diego also noticed a busking guitarist, with a portable amplifier, in one corner.

The busker moved on and Diego observed his patch beside the row of restaurants now lacking entertainment. He put a hand in his pocket and felt his meagre change, and thought, *Why not?* He strode over to the restaurants, removed his guitar from the case and instinctively laid the case open at his feet. Next, he plucked a chord of his guitar but the notes were lost in the voluminous space of the plaza. It was futile without an amp. Just as he was packing up, and about to return to the *taberna* and take the bar job, a man shouted from one table, "Hotel California, play us Hotel California."

The idea of playing feel-good melodies didn't appeal, but at that moment it seemed like an easy way to feed his belly. He collected his case, then stepped onto the restaurant's terrace. Diego nodded at a waiter standing in the doorway and he indicated with an approving smile that he was free to play there. Diego pulled his guitar close to his chest and began playing the song, but added a few flamenco twists. Afterwards, he received a warm round of applause from the diners as well as the waiting staff. A waiter passed him an empty beer glass and he went around the restaurant with it. Diego worked his way around the restaurants in that plaza, and within an hour he'd filled the glass with coins and Euro bills and found himself back at the first restaurant. He ordered a *caña* and it arrived with a bowl of complimentary olives.

As he tipped the money onto the table, the clinking of the coins brought to mind a moneybox he used to fill and hide under his bed as a child. It was made of metal and modelled on a pirate ship with a plastic swivel stopper underneath. Diego had imagined the ship sinking if he ever removed it. The coins he filled it with were the rewards for helping Papá on the candyfloss stall. Diego's job had been to add spoonfuls of coloured sugar into the machine's spinning drum, while his father continued dipping a stick and collecting the wispy clouds of candyfloss from it. And Papá would hand him a small coin for every sale they made. He also remembered those days being long; when they returned home he had to help clean the machine in the backyard before he was allowed to watch TV or practise the guitar.

Then, one day, when Diego was eight years old, he discovered he would soon have to sink his pirate ship. He and Papá had made a trip to Burgos and he'd spotted a little yellow bike in the shop window of a cycle shop. And he told himself he would soon buy that bike; then he would cycle to the next village, to the farm, now managed by his cousin Pedro. But he hadn't planned on stopping there for long, just time enough to collect some milk for the journey ahead. He had planned on cycling all the way to Madrid.

Why Madrid? Diego thought as he stared across the plaza. Then observing the glamorous plaza he remembered the images of the city on TV and in magazines that had dazzled the eyes of a young boy from a rural village. But surely there must have been more to it. Then it came to him; he had thought he might find his mother there.

Not long after Mamá's death, before his Papá had been affected by his moods of sullenness, Papá had tried to explain that Mamá's parting was like the life of the white butterfly. Many of the large butterflies hovered around the flowers in their backyard. He told Diego that they were the most beautiful creatures on the planet; although they only live for a few weeks, but during their short lives, they make many happy, by carrying pollen to flowers and making the world prettier. "That is why they are invited to heaven first," he had said. Heaven and death for a young boy had been an almost impossible concept to understand, and even though he'd attended his mother's funeral, Diego had pretended that she'd just gone away somewhere. And Madrid became that place, his substitute for heaven. To a village boy the stories and images of his country's capital were akin to a fantasy city and if you were beautiful like the butterflies, that is where you would disappear to.

But his dream of cycling to Madrid ended around the same time the flowers began to wilt and Papá began neglecting the house. Diego would often scramble under his bed to count the money, but one day his pirate ship was lost, and it was never found again. It wasn't until he was older he figured out it must have been his father who'd taken the money. He was the only other person who knew its hiding place. Even during their lean times Papá had always found money for a drink.

Diego took a sip of his beer, but he didn't feel any anger. He'd long forgiven his father for the money, he just felt sad. Then he spotted Mamadou and 'Watermelon Muscles' with other Africans, setting up a makeshift stall in the corner of the plaza, displaying fake-designer handbags and shoes. As he watched them setting up, he considered how precarious their lives must be. But he also thought about Mamadou's story and how he wasn't letting anything stand in the way of his dreams.

He ate another olive and finished his beer. Then, with his guitar under his arm, he headed across the plaza to greet Mamadou and the Africans. As he approached them, he noticed that Mamadou was the most proactive amongst the gang, engaging with an American woman who'd shown just a flicker of interest in one of the bags. His boyish grin dusted with charm from his touristy English was all it took to make the sale.

"Nice work!" exclaimed Diego, nodding at the Africans and reaching out a fist towards Mamadou.

"How you doin', brother?" replied Mamadou as he put out an open hand to shake Diego's.

He hastily uncurled his fingers and, as they shook hands in the way Diego was more familiar with, he suddenly felt very calm in Mamadou's company.

"Surviving," said Diego. "You know you have a gift."

"I do?"

"*Sí.*"

Mamadou, took out his comb and combed his Mohican. He took a few steps away from the gang, gesturing to Diego to follow. "Tell me more, brother."

Diego stepped closer to Mamadou and found himself whispering. "You're not afraid!"

Mamadou began laughing. "Oh, I've been plenty scared," he regained his composure and continued, "and I've avoided scrapes because of it. But fear can also be a drug if abused. It will always take the easy option. In Africa it was right to fear lions – they would come into our village and pick off a man just like that. It's such fear that led the village men to go off and hunt those lone predators that came prowling. Fear is about instinctive survival, it should never be used as an excuse not to seize an opportunity, however difficult it may seem."

"That's a great story but not everyone can be like you," said Diego as he thought of the flamenco school he hadn't entered. "What if you're not a good hunter and the lion corners you, then knocks your rifle out of your hand?"

Mamadou began laughing again. "That's your fault – if you're a lousy hunter you shouldn't have gone on the hunt. You leave hunting lions to those who are good at it. Perhaps your hunter should tune his instrument in preparation for the victorious hunters' return, if say music was his thing. His optimism would be better served for the celebration to come."

Diego removed his hat and wafted his face with it as he thought over Mamadou's words and said matter of factly, "You'll get your drumming school."

Mamadou's laughter lines looped into a smile. "I'll only have myself to blame if I don't."

Just then Mamadou spotted Daniel across the plaza and he waved towards him. Diego waved his hat. Daniel joined them and he explained he was out for an evening stroll. And he proposed they poke their heads into *Copas Anton*, the basement flamenco bar they'd visited on Friday night. Feeling happier after his talk with Mamadou and with some money in his pocket Diego accepted Daniel's proposal. And they left Mamadou with the Africans to continue working. And that was the start of Diego's routine for the next three weeks.

LATE AFTERNOON DIEGO would open the shutters and exit the apartment with his guitar hanging from a shoulder, supported by a shoulder strap that Daniel had fixed to the guitar with two pins. That way, Diego could easily duck in and out of the restaurants and bars without the need of an amp. And as he did his rounds, he'd often bump into Mamadou, 'Watermelons' and other Africans hawking their merchandise in the streets. They'd stop, chat and report where the best spot might be to ply their respective trades – the popular places with tourists that afternoon where they hadn't spotted any cops. Sometimes when Mamadou had his drum, Diego would play with him, and their music would help bring some extra trade and busking money. After playing, they would find a shady corner in the street and share their own experiences of growing up in a village, places so far away, though not so far apart in terms of the nature of the people that lived in them. Diego learned that everybody knew everyone's business in Mamadou's village, and like his, a lot of people had left for the cities and work. They could talk about anything; there were no taboos.

When Diego was done busking for the day, he'd head to *Copas Anton*. Anton was the owner, and namesake of his dingy bar.

During one night's drinking session in Anton's bar, there had been much debate about whom Diego had met when he'd mentioned his experience at *Arte del Flamenco*. Daniel, Anton and a regular couldn't agree who the female flamenco dancer must have been. Though they all knew the venue. It was a *peña* of old; traditionally only flamenco people were invited through the doors of such establishments, and it was always about the performance, never fancy food or cocktails. Though the quality and passion for flamenco were still strong in *Arte del Flamenco*, it was mainly tourist money that now kept it alive.

As for the choreographer, "You met Migolete, a flamenco master," Anton had said before giving the others a chance to correct him. He was now retired from dancing and was no longer spotted in the late flamenco bars, but anyone who'd watched flamenco in the 1980s would have known him well.

Frequently, the professional flamenco artists who went to *Copas Anton* after their shows would lead frenzied flamenco sessions into the early hours. After things calmed down and most people left, Diego would tell himself he'd never drink again, slump over to one of the tables and put his glass down on the frequently sticky surface. Then he'd take out his own guitar, experiment and practice the music he wasn't yet ready to share in the streets, imagining that was where his talent would be discovered. By the time he'd leave, the sun was often coming up.

8

Strings in the Shadows

Diego stepped out of the apartment building with his guitar in hand and immediately felt the heat. He looked up accusingly at the high August sun. It was mid-afternoon, the shadows were thin and there was nowhere to escape the sun's burning rays. The thought of another day's busking in the baking streets was nearly enough to send him back to his bed. Instead, he decided to take the day off. He returned his guitar to the apartment and as he walked back down the stairs he thought about what he might do for the afternoon. *A cold cerveza, in a shady plaza would be nice.* And he decided to contact Daniel about the idea. But then he remembered Daniel had just picked up a rare job and he didn't want to distract him from his work. During their evening drinking sessions, he'd listened kindly to Daniel's enthusiasm for carpentry and how it'd taken him a long time to realise it was the thing he liked most in life. And now he was devoted to being the best carpenter he could be and fulfilling his dream of having his own workshop one day. Then the idea struck Diego about visiting a luthier's guitar shop he'd spotted on his way home from *Copas Anton* one night.

It wasn't long before he reached the shaded backstreet where he believed the luthier's workshop was located. But the only shop he found was a tobacconist. Diego could have sworn it was there that he'd peered through the shop window, marvelling at the guitars on display.

Though he continued along the street, thinking it had to be around there somewhere. It wasn't looking promising and he had to acknowledge that the map in his head might be a little blurry. Further along, he eyed a metal sign with italic writing catching a shard of sunlight above the doorway. It read: *Rafael, Luthier.*

Diego strained his eyes as he looked through the window into a dark workshop. He saw cellos, violins, a double bass and a wooden workbench with various tools hanging behind it. He pressed his face against the window but still he couldn't see any guitars. He could have sworn on that night he'd viewed dozens of guitars in the shop in various stages of production and he particularly remembered one that reminded him of his father's. It must have been another shop. He pulled his face away from the glass and tried the shop's door handle but, as he expected, it was locked. No signage displayed the opening hours and Diego reckoned it was either closed for the *siesta* or for the summer holidays. He stepped back and looked further down the street, but there were no more shops, just rows of shuttered apartments.

He'd passed a *taberna* on the corner of the street and Diego decided he could ask in there if there was another guitar shop nearby, and also get something to eat. He walked back down the street and entered the bar. It had a fresh, bright feel to it, though it was traditional in style. Blue and white patterned mosaic tiles ran along the side of the bar counter and, sitting on top at one end, were tapas cabinets. Where pictures might have hung, bunches of chillies and garlic lined the walls. Off to one side of the bar was a busy dining room. Diego sat on a high stool at the bar and removed his hat. A barmaid with dark curly hair tied carelessly into a bun, and wearing a blue apron, glided passed him into the dining room with a tray of *cañas*. When she returned she smiled and took Diego's order.

He looked across to the tapas cabinet and ordered blood sausage, *padrón* peppers, Spanish *tortilla* and a *caña*. The woman served the food with a basket of small bread rolls. The meal tasted like heaven compared to the takeaway kebabs that he'd been living on recently. Much to his surprise, the peppers were sweeter and crunchier than the ones from home, and he picked at them slowly.

When he finished his food, he ordered another beer and asked the woman, "Is there a guitar *tienda* further along the street?"

"No, just the luthier's violin place a few doors down."

"That's strange? And there's no guitar shop nearby?"

"Not that I'm aware of."

The woman shrugged her shoulders as she tilted a glass under the beer tap and poured Diego his drink. She placed it on the bar and said, "The owner, Rafael, often comes in here later in the afternoon, perhaps he can solve your mystery?"

"If he does, can you introduce me?" replied Diego stretching a hand across the bar. "I'm Diego."

"*Con mucho gusto*, Diego," said the woman taking Diego's hand. "I'm Brenda."

Her hand felt hard like the calluses on the tips of his fingers contrasting markedly with her face, which was as smooth as the marbled surface of the counter.

Brenda went back into the dining room and Diego took a sip of his beer. Then he got down from the stool and went outside to have a smoke. Smoking he gazed along the narrow street and the alleyways leading off it. He'd done well maintaining his stamina; keeping up the busking in the afternoons through to the night, then whiling away his time in *Copas Anton* but always working on his music before he left the place and walked off the alcohol on his way home. Even so, it was good to have a day off. He figured his repertoire of songs were now a hundred or so and at least half of them were original. But there was something missing in what he was doing, and he wasn't sure what it was.

When he finished his cigarette, he decided he should leave; knowing it'd be too easy to order another beer and stay there for the rest of the day. Just then a portly man with glasses dangling around his neck strolled up to the *taberna*. He had silver shoulder-length hair, a thick beard and was wearing a white linen shirt. The man nodded courteously at Diego before he brushed through the beaded curtains and went into the *taberna*. Diego had the feeling this man was the luthier. He stubbed out his cigarette and went back inside. The man had taken a stool in the middle of the bar, besides Diego's spot. Diego tried his best not to stare and sat back down.

"How are you today?" asked Brenda.

"*Muy bien*; it's beautiful *señoritas* like you that keep old men like me happy."

Brenda smiled, "*Carajillo*?"

"You know me too well, Brenda."

Brenda gestured towards Diego. "Rafael let me introduce you to Diego."

"*Con mucho gusto*, Diego," said Rafael.

"Likewise," replied Diego with an extended nod. "*Carajillo* was always my Papá's drink of choice as well."

"The best drink there is for working men," Rafael said wryly as he noted Brenda adding the rum to his black coffee.

"Guess so," replied Diego.

Brenda placed the glass on the bar beside Rafael, and he immediately took a couple of sips, oblivious to the sharpness Diego imagined it would have.

"So did you take after your Papá?" said Rafael putting his glass down.

"I'm more of a *cerveza* man," replied Diego with a grin.

"No, I meant are you a working man?" said Rafael glancing at Diego's Stetson on the bar.

"Sorry, I knew what you meant. Well, you might say I'm a working guitarist, I'm busking on the streets. But I want to really make it as a professional flamenco guitarist."

Rafael nodded subtly as if giving Diego approval to speak his mind, and he continued talking.

"When I was young, Papá encouraged me to play the guitar, but when my mother passed away, when I was just a kid, he lost his enthusiasm for everything including the guitar."

"That's tough," interjected Rafael knowingly. "Some people never get over losing the love of their life."

"It was only towards the end that he seemed to accept everything. You see he died recently. Just before he died, he had one of those talks with me. You know, a father to son sort of thing about living your life and not making his mistakes. He'd never spoken to me like that before. Then he pushed me out the door, and it's because of him I'm now trying to make a success of things with the guitar. But in this city, although I'm only twenty-two, I feel it's too late for me. I'm not formally trained, never played at flamenco festivals, nor auditioned anywhere. You know how some football players are groomed from an early age by the professional clubs, but many talented players are overlooked if they don't follow that route and go on to work jobs that never really satisfy them, and they end up jealous and unhappy."

"Condolences for your recent loss, but let me ask you, do you believe that playing the guitar is your gift?"

Diego took a sip of beer and sighed, "*Sí,* but maybe that's not enough in this world?"

"Life is hard, but we all have a gift for something, and you're still young and have time. Take any job if it means paying the bills and playing every day. But don't ever think about reaching perfection or being frustrated by not getting there, because one's great work is never totally finished. For example, others might look at a viola I have crafted and think it is magnificent, but in my mind's eye, I'd be thinking I could have done better, made the sound slightly sharper or rounded its curves with a little more panache. But if you always think that way you will never improve and move on to your next piece."

Diego raised his glass at Rafael. "*Gracias* for sharing that with me, but can I ask have you ever struggled as a luthier?"

"All talented people struggle at times, that's life. I am not alone but when you stop believing, that's when you're defeated. You talk of the footballers who've been nurtured all the way. But they've all experienced losses of form. Though the great players, when they suffer from this, work harder in training, and never lose faith. Who's your team?"

"*Barca*,"

"Well, even the great Messi has had periods where he hasn't scored for several games. Then everyone is quick to write him off, saying he's lost his magic, but he always comes back with wonderful goals."

"That's true, but I always believed he would."

"*Sí*, because you recognise someone who is living his gift, who has continued faith."

It's *inori*, thought Diego, but he didn't say it.

"And when did you struggle?" asked Diego

"When I first bought my workshop."

"The one, up the street with the violins?"

"*Sí*, that's it. Business was poor in the early days; it took time for my reputation to spread, and previously it'd been a luthier and *tienda* of flamenco guitars, so people kept coming to my shop expecting to find guitars."

"Really?" said Diego.

Rafael took a sip from his glass and said, "I spent most of my time directing people to where the previous guitar business had moved to. It was frustrating, but I always knew I'd done the right thing going it alone and setting up there. That was some thirty years ago and I'm still going."

"And you've never worked on guitars?"

"Never."

"That's really strange because one night I was looking through your window and I could have sworn I saw guitars in there," said Diego.

"Sometimes, when I work late, I hear the folk flamenco of old. The first time I heard the music I wondered if I'd drunk too much rum, but the sound was very crisp, strings of the finest guitars. And now, when I've had a little too much to drink and I'm incapable of working, I put my tools down and play the violin; and if I'm lucky the guitars return to the shop and forgive me for my bad playing and accompany me. I think of them as the old *amigos* I've lost touch with or have passed on. So what do you think, should they have me committed for hearing things?"

"I guess I'm no more mad than you are. I peered through your window and perhaps I was seeing the guitars that you hear. Unless my drunk mind believed I was looking at guitars when in fact they were violins?"

"No, I'd say you've got a good eye for a guitar. People once came from all over the world to buy flamenco guitars from those premises. I believe some of the guitars never wanted to leave that building; it was a magical place."

Momentarily, Diego closed his eyes to think and thereafter said, "Not long ago a luthier in León mentioned my father's guitar was made in Madrid. What was the name of the guitar business that was once there?"

"*Guitarras Ramirez.*"

"That's it, that's who the luthier said made it. He suggested the guitar was made at the time of the civil war."

"Your father fought in the civil war?"

"*Sí*, he did."

"He must have been very old when he fathered you?"

"He was; people often mistook him as my grandfather."

"Perhaps you saw your father's old guitar through my shop window; echoes of our past lives are always around us, and sometimes they show up in the most unexpected of places. The Ramirez business outgrew the workshop, but some of its memories are still engrained there."

"Maybe," said Diego wistfully.

"Your father was a Republican soldier then?"

"He was, a very young one," Diego found himself saying proudly.

"The worst of times and the best of times, they say. Madrid was under siege for nearly three years – it would have brought the best out of a flamenco guitarist at the time." Rafael became exultant. "Agh, to have lived then!" He cast his eyes across the bar and cried, "Get this man a *cerveza*, and I'll join him in one."

Brenda looked up from where she was washing glasses and raised her eyebrows.

"*Sí*, I'll have a *cerveza*!"

Brenda shrugged her shoulders and proceeded to pull their drinks.

"You'll join me?"

"*Gracias*," replied Diego.

"I'm told this was one of the places to come for a fiesta then. Perhaps your papá once brought some merriment to his comrades in this very same *taberna*."

Brenda placed their drinks in front of them and Rafael raised his glass. "I propose a toast."

"What are we toasting?"

"How about to your papá?"

Diego smiled and he raised his glass and they said, "¡*Salud!*" in unison.

An idea came into Rafael's head as he drank his beer. He called back Brenda and asked, "Do you have any of those old photos that used to hang on the walls?"

Diego eyed Brenda curiously as she thought for a moment, then she said, "They're probably in the cellar," and smiled. "Can I trust you both not to drink the place dry if I take a look?"

"Best be quick," replied Rafael, glancing at Diego with a grin.

Brenda left the bar and disappeared through a door in the dining area and soon returned with a box. And as they looked through black and white framed photos of various flamenco artists and people who had once frequented the place, Brenda explained to Diego that the *taberna* had passed down through the various generations of her family. And many of the photos they were looking at had been taken during the time her grandfather ran it. As a girl, she'd listened to his stories from the war and how he fought to keep the bar open.

And during the aerial bombardments by the Nationalists, the bar would move down to the cellar and Grandpapa opened the bar's doors to those neighbours who had nowhere to shelter. The bombing made it impossible to sleep and the flamenco people in the cellar did their best to distract everyone with improvised jigs and singing. Brenda's grandpapa had often referred to one man; a Republican soldier, who'd been little more than a boy, and had played the flamenco guitar in their cellar during those times. He had a gift for finding the right lilts to lift everyone's spirits. And with children, he always managed to strike a special accord; plucking strings in a playful way that brought smiles and laughter to their faces.

Grandpapa would talk with affection about the various characters that frequented the *taberna* in his time, and he'd always wondered what had happened to that boy-soldier after the war.

After Brenda recalled the story, Rafael played with his beard and beheld Diego with kind-hearted eyes, as if hinting that the boy-soldier Brenda had mentioned in the story may in fact have been his papá. Diego rejected that idea with dismissive eyes. It was a tale too far to believe.

Diego continued flicking through the photos and suddenly one held his gaze. In the photo he saw a young man, with a wide childlike grin, standing with his back against a bar counter and resting an elbow on its shiny marble top. In his other hand, he held a guitar by its neck. The guitar was not yet darkened with age, but Diego knew it instantly. It was a guitar he'd journeyed with – it was his papá's old guitar. The youthful man had the same dark eyes as his father but a thick mop of hair. Diego's hand began to shake. He looked up at Rafael and Brenda and they both understood he had found a photo of his papá, leaning against the very same bar counter they were now sitting at.

I should have known, Papá had always loved children, Diego thought. *Why else would he have had a candyfloss cart!* Then he recalled the words that his father had said to him in the bedroom that last night before he'd died, "During my time selling candyfloss, I made a million smiles."

Diego shivered.

"Take the photo," said Brenda.

"I can have it?"

Brenda smiled and Diego didn't ask again. He placed it on the bar beside his beer. Then he finished it off in a couple of glugs and asked, "Can I buy you both a drink?"

"*Gracias*, but no," said Rafael. "I've already had too much, God knows what kind of racket I'll be making in my workshop tonight with my violin."

And Brenda replied, "I never drink on the job," and dried a glass with a tea towel and added with a smile, "That would be ruinous."

"In that case, I'll be on my way," said Diego. "Brenda, *la cuenta por favor*."

Brenda picked up another glass up and wiping it smiled. "I'll add it to your papá's bar tab."

Diego didn't argue with her, her smile was all-consuming; instead, he got down from the stool, put his hat on and picked up the framed photo.

"Well, I'll see you around," said Diego, stretching out a hand to Rafael.

But Rafael didn't meet his hand with his and instead raised his beer glass to Diego as Brenda said, "We're always here," before she collected another glass to dry.

Diego smiled back at them, turned and left the bar. His hand felt numb as he carried the photo and walked back to the apartment. He was happy to think his papá, had had some youthful secrets, but he wished he'd known him better.

When he arrived at the door of his apartment block, a black cat with white paws stretched across the doorway in a patch of sun. It looked at Diego with wary green eyes but didn't move. Diego stepped over it, into the building and climbed the stairs to the apartment. Upon entering, the first thing he did was to wrap the photo in a newspaper, along with the framed photo of his mother his father had given him at the outset of his journey, before placing the parcel deep into his backpack. Then he took a nap to sleep off the beer and settle his emotions.

9

Mari

D iego awoke fresh that evening and went onto the balcony to take in the air of the city. Lights were flickering across the night, and the cross on a nearby church steeple flared incandescently. The night was full of possibilities as Diego grabbed his guitar and left the apartment for *Copas Anton*. Upon arriving, he briefly joined Daniel and two men at the bar, but when Daniel offered Diego a beer, to everyone's surprise, he replied, "No *gracias amigo*. Just a *café solo*." And with that he patted his friend on the back and found himself a quiet corner.

Diego placed the guitar in his lap, brushed the strings with his strumming hand and went to work on a tune that had been frustrating him for some time. The melody came like the season of spring, raw to begin with, though softening, occasionally broken by intermittent hauntings of the recent past; before a wide range of vibrant notes broke free of any winter bleakness. Diego didn't dwell on the tune, instead he moved on to other complicated arrangements. The tunes jerked, splintered and rattled. But they also found their way.

Happy with his work, Diego went up to the bar to drink his now tepid coffee. He made small talk and, when he'd finished his coffee, the two regulars tried their best to persuade him to remain in their drinkers' circle. For a moment, he hesitated, though Daniel gestured at the photo of Paco de Lucía on the wall. Diego smiled optimistically back at his friend and went back to his corner and continued his practice session. Diego surprised himself at his progress; but he wasn't the only one surprised, someone from her own corner had found his music arresting.

She'd been keeping a cautious eye on Diego ever since their first encounter in the bar; when she'd urged him to show her what he could do with the guitar. But before he had snapped the guitar string, she'd thought she'd glimpsed something special in him. However, during his return visits, she'd observed Diego was much like other men who frequented late night bars. But now she saw him sitting alone and holding his guitar in quiet devotion. He was handsome, and his eyes were blind to everything beyond the strings of his guitar, beyond the music he pictured in the darkness.

Diego didn't sing but if he'd added lyrics to one of the melodies he was composing he imagined it might have gone something like this:

Not cast stones on water
Gaze in puddles after rain
But 'tis always in vain.

I follow the rainbows,
Take me home hopeful days.
Just Papá snoring, asleep,
Bottle and broach his keepsake.

Hair glittering,
Butterfly shimmering,

Candle always flickering
Mamá?

When Diego was done, he went up to the counter, ordered a *caña* and joined his friends. And the woman discovered herself getting up from her table and slinking in beside Diego at the corner of the bar counter. Although Diego felt her warmth, he kept his back to her and remained sipping his beer. He asked Daniel how his day had gone working on the new carpentry job he'd picked up, and Daniel began explaining he'd been making some new legs for a table. Diego had hoped the conversation with his friend would be enough to divert him from the woman beside him but the problem was that he'd had his eye on her since their chance meeting.

She ordered vermouth, but after taking a couple of sips from her glass she became impatient and nudged into Diego. Vermouth splashed onto the sleeve of his shirt.

"I'm sorry, did I spill any of my drink on you?" she asked innocently.

Diego glanced at his sleeve and then at Daniel who raised his eyebrows back at him in response.

"It's just a drop, no sweat," replied Diego as he turned to face the woman.

"That's good," she responded, flicking her fringe to one side.

Though he'd noticed her dark eyes before, now he also saw a light in them, shining strange and intensely in her oval face. And faded creases at the corners of her mouth ran down to her jawline. Diego's eyes were then drawn to the outline of her cleavage bursting up through the top of her black, low-cut dress, and suddenly mindful she might catch him out, he shifted them upwards and grinned. "And your drink missed my boyfriend," he said running a hand over the curved shoulder of his guitar.

She began laughing. "You must really like him – you didn't break any of his strings tonight."

"I'm learning to be less rough with the sensitive types."

"That's sensible; all musicians are very sensitive."

"And you? Are you the sensitive type?"

"Of course, I'm a dancer. It's a tough life you know," she replied, tempering her laughter.

"Why do you say that?"

"There's a lot of bullshit and politics that goes with it."

"You can't get away from politics in Spain. Well that, and religion, or at least that's what my father used to say. Still to get paid to perform your art, your gift; something that you must have trained a long time for that's special, no? And as a dancer don't you get to tour and travel sometimes?"

She took a sip of her vermouth, composing her response. "It can be very tiring, the rehearsals, late nights. Yes, I've attended festivals and gone on the road with shows. But you rarely have time to see much beyond the concert halls and hotels. I would love to travel, to really take the time to visit places. And to be honest, I'm not sure dancing is my thing."

"But you're good?"

"*Sí* but I've trained for a long time. And I'm always playing to the tune of someone else's fiddle, the choreographers'."

Diego leaned against the bar and took a drink of his beer, then said, "I'm sure it would be amazing to see you dance."

"Okay," she replied. "How about now?"

Confusion flashed across Diego's face.

"I mean everyday dancing – let's go to a nightclub."

"I'm not much of a dancer, but why not?" he said, rubbing his guitar again. "I've never gotten much practice, given her wooden hip and all."

"I thought it was a he?" she said laughing.

Diego winked. "I'm very open-minded. Okay, give me a minute." He turned to Daniel and nodded subtly towards the woman beside him. "I'll catch up with you tomorrow. Err, we're going to check out a club."

Daniel grinned back at Diego. "Enjoy yourself *amigo*."

Diego turned his attention back to the dancer. "By the way, I'm Diego."

"I know."

"You do?"

"*Sí*, I asked one of your friends a while back," she said, holding out a slender hand.

"I'm Mari."

Diego took hold of it and her hand felt as smooth as a silk glove. He grabbed Anton's attention and passed him his guitar across the bar for safekeeping. Then Diego left the bar with Mari.

∾

DIEGO RAN UP the stairs, just ahead of her, and reaching the third floor he raised his arms like a jubilant athlete and shouted, "*¡Campeón, campeón!*"

Mari arrived behind him. "I would have won, but you cheated?" she said laughing.

"How's that?" Diego said, catching his breath.

"I was laughing too much."

"Come on, Mari," said Diego with a smile. "That's not my fault."

"Absolutely it is!"

"¿*Cómo*?"

"You're so funny, so serious about winning."

"Am I?"

Mari opened the door to her apartment and cocked her head at Diego, beckoning him in. He followed, and as she turned on a floor lamp, the first thing Diego noticed in the front room was a large canvas painting of a black ballet dancer mounted above a round dining table. The painting depicted the dancer sitting on a wooden chair in front of a studio mirror. Her forearms rested on her thighs, over a long, white sequined dress, and she had an absent expression. On the other side of the room, there was a desk stacked with books, magazines and make-up. There was also a small sofa, with some dresses scattered across it, against a wall with wooden windows. A small Moroccan rug covered the middle of the parquet flooring and there were more books piled up on the floor. The apartment was old but had a cosy feel to it.

Mari placed her keys on the desk, then walked slowly towards Diego. She curled her hands around his neck and they were kissing again. They had danced slowly in that position earlier in the nightclub and they'd talked in a corner of the club and Mari shared her story of why she'd always wanted to be a flamenco dancer. For as long as she could remember, there had been a flamenco dancer on the mantelpiece of her grandmother's house.

And to a small girl, the doll had looked like a princess, in its white dress with blue ruffles, and a rose in its hair. Though later in the night Mari had revealed her flamenco life was a strange existence. She didn't have any real friends outside of her flamenco circles and she wanted to get away from it for a while. And Diego had shared his recent story, including the passing of his father, and Mari had listened with much fascination, desire growing.

They stopped kissing and Mari led Diego into her bedroom. She turned on a lamp on the bedside table and a pedestal fan, and they undressed in the pale light and fell gently into the bed. They held each other under the sheet and for a moment it felt enough; two strangers in need of human contact although they had gotten used to their own space. But Diego felt Mari shudder as the fan breezed across her shoulders and he gently squeezed her. She felt the heat of Diego's body and wanted it to envelope her and she pulled him on top of her. He felt her breathing, observed her hair flaring as shadows on the wall and the bridge of his feet connected with the arches of hers. He worked his lips down her body and Mari opened her legs and closed her eyes. Then she was no longer in the room; she was lying in a straw field, her body prickly and sensitive. The sky was a watery pale blue, with wispy horsetail clouds and she arched her pelvis, dug her fingers into Diego's lower back and drew him in. Their senses aligned; primordial, harmonious, unfathomable. After they held each other tightly, still and wordless. Until, at some point in the night, the darkness pulled them to their own sides of the bed and they fell into a deep sleep.

The clattering of bottles and the engine of a recycling truck woke them in the early morning, and they nestled together for a minute, before making love again. For the first time in his life, Diego didn't feel compelled to untangle his body and escape from the woman he'd woken up next to. Though Mari felt nervous for giving herself a second time to someone she hardly knew and she slid out of the bed and went into the bathroom.

When she returned, she was wearing a white bathrobe and asked: "You like coffee?"

Diego winked. "It's nearly the best way to start the day!"

"Okay," she said quietly, turning and leaving the room.

At that moment, everything felt less complicated to Diego and the notion to think how he might express the evening, how he might recall it later and reinterpret it into another song, didn't seem to matter. He sat upright, puffed a pillow behind his back and waited without a thought.

Mari returned a few minutes later with a tray containing a French press, a jug of milk, cups and a packet of cereal cookies. And she gave the tray to Diego to hold as she climbed on top of the bed.

"A man could get used to this," he said, balancing the tray between them.

"Well don't get too used to it – I've got rehearsals this morning," replied Mari plunging the coffee press.

Mari poured the coffees and handed Diego a cup, and Diego added milk to his and Mari gestured to him to add some to her own cup.

Her phone vibrated on the table beside her, so she put her cup down on the table and picked up the phone. She glanced at the text message she'd received and put the phone back down.

"My mother. She's always checking up on me now," claimed Mari. She hesitated as if she wasn't ready to reveal something about life. "And what about your mother?"

Diego took a sip of coffee, then replied, "She died when I was very young, so there's not much to say. I only have few memories of her, but I do know she did make my papá very happy."

Mari took a sip of her coffee and Diego continued, "She had small hands like yours. They're what I see most of in my recollections of her. I remember her peeling white asparagus. I'd just started school and Papá used to bring me home, and some of those afternoons, she'd be there waiting and sitting on a small stool, peeling the asparagus in our backyard. She was very methodical – snapping the stalks and drawing the knife up the stems with her hands. I think she used to wear an apron, but in my memory, I see her in brightly coloured floral dresses. It's funny, I don't recall her peeling any other vegetables."

"That's a nice memory," said Mari, handing Diego a cookie. "You're very sensitive really, underneath it all."

"Didn't you say all musicians are last night?" Diego smiled shyly and took a bite of the cookie.

"Yes – all of them! It's not always easy working with musicians. Actually, I wasn't sure if I should mention it," continued Mari. "But I was thinking that there might be an opening for you. An *amigo*, the director of a new flamenco show, has been holding auditions in one of the city's theatres. He's got most people he needs, but he hasn't found the right lead guitarist. He's very particular, but you could be just what he's looking for. I can contact him today, if you like?"

Diego chewed on the biscuit, then asked, "It's going to be a big show?"

"It's an artsy kind of studio theatre in *barrio* La Latina. It wouldn't be high-paying, but you'd make some great contacts, and it would be very convenient for you."

"*Claro*, well if I get the job."

"That's down to you, but an audition I can get you. I've worked with the director several times," said Mari, putting her cup on the tray and handing it to Diego. "I need to get on."

Mari stepped off the bed and avoiding Diego's hand reaching out to pull her back, said, "I'll phone him after I've showered," and left the room.

Diego topped up his coffee, thinking Mari wasn't a drinker and he'd have to adapt his drinking habits if he wanted to spend more time with her. He knew she would be impressed if he could get this new gig. And he started to imagine them performing at their respective shows and meeting up after, just for a drink or two to share their day's gossip before leaving together. Or if he finished before her, he'd race across town and surprise her by catching the end of her performance.

Mari returned to the room wearing her bathrobe. Her hair was wet and tangled. She reached for a wooden hairbrush on top of the chest of drawers, and began brushing out the knots. "I left you a blue towel in the bathroom," she said, nodding towards the bedroom door.

Diego put the tray on the floor and, with a grin, he reached for his Stetson, got out of bed and swept the hat in front of his body like a matador might do with a cape, before hiding his private parts with the hat. Mari grinned, and picked up a hairdryer, as Diego collected his clothes and left the room.

He showered, dressed quickly, and went into the lounge-diner. Mari was sitting at her desk writing on a Post-it note. She was still wearing the bathrobe but her hair was now glossy and dry.

"It's fixed," she said, looking up and handing Diego the Post-it.

Diego looked at the note and the information Mari had scribbled. She'd written: '6pm' and '*Francis*', and his phone number.

"*Gracias*," he said, putting the Post-it in a pocket. "Six o'clock today?"

"*Sí*. Francis is keen to meet you. There's only one theatre in La Latina – you can't miss it; it's beside the Metro entrance."

Mari picked up her phone and handed it to Diego, "Type in your number and pass me your phone."

Diego smiled and gave Mari his phone and they entered their respective numbers into each other's devices before returning them.

"Are you free later?" asked Diego.

"I don't think it's going to be possible today. We're choreographing a difficult move, which yesterday wasn't going so well and tonight I'm performing at the *tablao* I mentioned."

"Oh, okay,"

"But text me after the audition and let me know how it went. Tomorrow would be much better to meet up," said Mari, standing up and reaching her arms around Diego.

They held each other and kissed for a minute before Mari pulled away.

"Go, go, Diego, before you make me late," Mari said with a smile.

And before Diego knew it, he was standing outside Mari's doorway, waiting for the lift. He listened to the mechanism of cogs and cables creaking as the lift wound its way up to his floor and when it arrived, he reluctantly stepped into the confined space.

Diego hadn't paid much attention to where Mari lived on their way back from the club the previous night, he had been caught up in the excitement of the evening. But when he stepped out into her street, he sensed he was in the centre still. After a short walk, he soon discovered himself on a pedestrianised shopping boulevard, a place he'd once busked before. Doors and shutters of stores rattled open and Diego eyed a shaded café terrace and a couple of old men sitting outside it. He considered drinking a *carajillo* there to help settle his pre-audition nerves. However, he felt a little sick and instead continued along the street in the direction of his apartment.

Diego had the same sinking feeling he used to have before sitting exams. He tried to distract himself by thinking about what might have been if he'd studied and taken those final exams. And he remembered that his refusal to do so had also been about provoking his father. A test of sorts, one he thought his father had failed at. When word had got back that Diego didn't show up for those exams, Papá hadn't said much. He'd just stood up from his chair in front of the television, thought for a moment then said, "Well, school didn't do me much good." Subsequently he'd sat back down and changed the channel to the news.

When Diego arrived back at the apartment block, the black cat was again outside, but it was now a metre or so away, stretching out in the sun, avoiding the shadow of the building. He opened the front door and climbed the dark stairs to the apartment. Inside, he pulled off his boots and sat on the bed with the idea of resting a little. Thoughts raced around in his head. Would he have to perform his own music or an audition piece? Would he have to read music or accompany someone? What if others were auditioning and they asked him about where he had trained? It was a competitive business he was learning, and they might catch him out. It was pointless trying to sleep with these anxieties, so he decided to tidy the apartment.

The apartment was spotless by the time he was done. Next Diego showered and, to his surprise, found a clean, black T-shirt in his backpack and put it on. He ate cornflakes from the box and, just as he was finishing them, he realised he hadn't seen his guitar anywhere. Then he remembered he'd left it with Anton at the bar. He checked the time on his phone, it was just after 17:00; he had less than an hour to collect his guitar and make it to the audition. Diego quickly pulled on his boots and shot out of the apartment.

He hot-footed it across the centre and, after banging loudly on the door of *Copas Anton* several times, Anton opened the door, returned his guitar and gave him a *caña* to see him on his way. Diego drank it down in three thirsty gulps, wedged his guitar under his arm and raced across the old town. And he arrived at the theatre on the dot of six o'clock. He was shown to a chair on the stage. With the glow of the stage lights on him, he couldn't see much beyond the first row of seats and the man he was auditioning for. Diego caught his breath, sat down, adjusted his hat and studied Francis. He was holding a clipboard and wearing round-framed glasses, giving him the look of a student, although an amber bald patch on the crown of his head suggested he was older. Francis shifted the bridge of his glasses so they rested on the front of his nose, and eyed Diego from above. Then he explained what he wanted.

The audition was over in a puff, and Diego had taken himself to the theatre's bar to think it over more clearly. He bought a large glass of beer and stood outside the entrance in a sun that felt hotter than usual that evening, placing his glass on an old wine barrel. Francis had outlined the story of the musical: a tale of the cycle of life as evident through the friendship of two men now in their autumn years. The entire musical would be devoted to a retirement fiesta, whereby one of the friends, a flamenco singer, performs his final *cante*, a song about deception, choices, loves lost and nature. Diego's audition had been to play a tune on his strings that he felt best represented the mood of that final song the director had described.

After Diego had performed, Francis had become agitated and all Diego could see of him in the dark auditorium was his shining bald spot as he paced up and down anxiously. Unsure what to do, Diego stayed put, awaiting a decision. But when Francis had found his composure, he returned to the front row and soberly said, "You're fantastic, but a name sells tickets." He hadn't said much more; Diego had received a warm handshake and that had been that.

He lifted his beer off the barrel and drank it down, exasperated, believing he'd just played the best performance of his life, and that there was nothing more he could have given Francis. It all seemed a game and Flamenco's hierarchy changed the rules as they saw fit. In his disappointment, he had not yet texted Mari, and now Diego's only thought was to see her. The idea suddenly struck him that maybe he'd be able to catch Mari, that night, either before or after her evening show. *Make this your last drink*, he thought. He took his phone out of a pocket and sent Mari a text:

@}->---

Tilting his phone and squinting at the emoji he had created, he wondered if Mari would understand it was a rose. He glanced at his guitar leaning against the barrel and whispered, "What would you have said?" Diego raised his empty glass at the guitar.

"*¡Salud!*" he said aloud. "You wouldn't care; you'd just keep playing your damn music!"

He leaned against the barrel and composed another text:

The bad news is I didn't get the theatre gig but the good news is I now have more time to get to know you ;)

Diego didn't receive a reply to his message, so he decided to buy himself another beer to distract himself whilst he waited for one. When he came back from the bar, he drank his beer greedily and, when he had finished it, there was still no response from Mari so he sent her another text:

Why the radio silence??

He went inside again and ordered himself a rum and coke this time. Back outside, the streets were becoming busy with people returning from work. He viewed a young executive buying a newspaper at a tobacconist – the sheen of his suit shimmered in the lowering sun. Diego couldn't help but feel jealous; thinking the man's position in life had probably been taken care of by his family from an early age: private schooling, college and business contacts, no doubt. Anxiety and alcohol mixed in Diego's head, swelling into a cocktail of rage and envy. He felt the need to have some consistency, to have some regular money, to fend off the feeling of panic that was suddenly bubbling up through his mind. Again he picked up the phone and proceeded to tap out another text and, for a second, his index finger hovered over the send button as he re-thought the wording:

It's bad manners not to respond!?

He immediately regretted sending it. Diego sipped his drink and stared blankly across the street at the drinkers and diners at a busy café terrace as well as people going in and out of the metro entrance. He was a lone disconnected figure, like a wax cowboy in a museum. Eventually he snapped out of his reverie, finished his drink and stepped away from the terrace with just one purpose in mind, to see Mari.

Swifts skimmed across the upper balconies of white buildings and flew higher to merge with the darkening sky. Just as Diego was about to reach for his phone again, he felt it vibrate and there was a message from Mari:

Sorry about the audition but there will be others. And gracias for the rose.

Then another message came through:

But you confuse me? I want a man who respects me and doesn't act like a child when I don't immediately reply. I said I'd be busy rehearsing – do you allow yourself to be distracted when you're mastering a song?

Diego read the message twice and just as he was working out a response he received a third text:

When I've had time to think about this I will get in touch. Until then be well and please do not contact me. Buenos noches. Mari

With darkening eyes, he read the message and checked the time, it was 20:32. *There's still time*, he thought, *to catch her performing*. Momentarily, he considered this might be a bad idea. But he felt lonely and desperately wanted to see Mari. He'd apologise for his last text and she'd see the sincerity in his face, then he would put his cards on the table and state his affection for her. He put his phone away and swayed a little as he paced through the busy streets on the way to the *tablao* at which she'd told him she was currently performing. He knew the place having passed it during his busking outings.

The *tablao* was in the centre of town, and he soon arrived outside its wide doors. They swung open and a couple, arm-in-arm, came out. Diego spied an internal glass door and an amber haze beyond. He entered and pushed open the glass door and stepped through to the flamenco club. The maître d', a tall man, in a sharp suit and wearing designer glasses, squinted at Diego, before his attention was distracted by the arrival of a large party. The echoing hands of *palmeros* turned Diego's head to a stage of whirling dancers in folk dress. Then he spotted Mari – sitting with musicians at the back of the stage.

He glanced back at the maître d', but he was busy greeting the guests and showing them to their table. Diego shrugged his shoulders and casually walked over to the back of the club to the bar. He pulled out a stool and waved at the barman. But his signal went unnoticed as the man was at the far end of the bar busily preparing drinks orders for the anxious table waiters to dispatch. Diego leaned over the counter and spied a bottle of rum and swiped it, while with his other hand, he reached for a glass and surreptitiously filled it. The barman continued to be distracted by a flurry of waiters needing drinks for their customers and Diego continued to help himself to the rum until the moment Mari took centre stage, and he was mesmerised. He eyed her all the way up from the heels of her shoes, curved like the arches of a bridge, across her willowy body swirling in a blood red dress, along her slender neck and up to her motherly eyes. Her limbs moved with the agility of the wings of a bird. Diego wanted to hover beside her, and see the world as she did at that moment.

The rest of the show passed in a blur and when Mari and the performers finished and bowed Diego got down from the stool, steadied himself against the bar, and began clapping and cheering, "*Bravo, bravo,*" but to his disappointment, Mari didn't appear to notice him. The performers left the stage through a door marked, *Privado*, and Diego felt the urge to follow behind them.

He took a step towards it but the maître d' shot across the room and blocked his path, firstly nodding towards the bar where Diego had been drinking freely and next he gestured at a security man.

Diego didn't say a word as the security man led him to the doorway and threw him onto the street. He didn't feel the stone paving, all he sensed was the hazy glow of a lamp. Sometime later, somebody lifted him to his feet and propped him up against the shutters of a shop. Diego's focus returned and he observed in front of him a man holding out his guitar; it was the guitarist with the goatee who'd been with Mari that first night in *Copas Anton.*

He pushed the guitar into Diego's arms and turned away towards a small group of people standing under the light of a nearby streetlamp. As he walked away he glanced over his shoulder and said, "Her ex-husband was an alcoholic."

Under the lamp, Diego could see the outline of Mari, but within a moment she and the group were gone and had submerged into the night. For a while, he gazed at the light and the black dots of insects entranced around its haze. Before he wrapped an arm around the neck of his guitar and staggered off. And in the dark alleys, Diego and his guitar might have been mistaken for two drunks propping each other up.

10

The Pilgrim

Diego stood smoking on the balcony, watching birds circling across the red rooftops. He'd woken up late the next afternoon after a fitful sleep. His head throbbed, his throat stung and already the day was lost in his mind. All he wanted to see were the patchy fields of home. "*¡Puta!*" he exclaimed aloud. "Why did I do that?" He tried to be resolute and convince himself that that was the last of this drinking, but he didn't really believe it, drinking had always been his default option when he was having a bad day. His mind returned to the hazy scene of limping through the nocturnal streets the night before, entering *Copas Anton* and declaring with a holler what a vile place Madrid was. Next, like a madman he'd raised his guitar high above his head and slammed it onto the floor.

After crashing the guitar, all he remembered were Paco's big eyes glaring at him from out of the photo frame and ascending the steps to the street. He assumed he'd left the broken guitar in the basement bar, as he hadn't seen it in the apartment. *I am capable of much stupidity*, he thought. His brooding was interrupted by his phone ringing. He stubbed out his cigarette, tossed it over the balcony and dashed into the bedroom. Diego grabbed the phone desperately hoping it was Mari.

But it was Daniel. He asked Diego how he was feeling, as he'd been at *Copas Anton* and witnessed his impromptu performance. Daniel was worried about him and persuaded Diego to meet him in an hour's time. Though all Diego really wanted to do was to go back to bed then quietly leave Madrid the next morning to return home. Smashing his guitar had been a declaration that it was all over. It was a waste of time attending more auditions in a city where the rules of the game were not suited to him.

A long shower helped Diego get himself together and leave the apartment. He walked lazily to the plaza Daniel told him about and he spotted him relaxing at a table in the café's busy terrace, smoking and drinking a *caña*. Leaning against the table was Daniel's guitar case.

"*Hola*," said Diego sheepishly.

Daniel looked up. "*Buenas tardes amigo*," he said with a smile.

Diego pulled out a chair and sat down. "*¿Qué pasa?*"

"Been busy, now relaxing."

"You've been busking?" said Diego, nodding at the guitar.

"No. Perhaps later? It's Saturday after all."

"Oh," replied Diego.

"A *cerveza* might do the trick," said Daniel oddly. "Do you think?"

"How do you manage it?" replied Diego, glancing at Daniel's beer glass.

"I'm a better drinker than you, or maybe it's because I always leave before you do? Though you didn't hang around last night, not even to take a bow. That was quite a performance. Where had you been before?"

Diego wanted to share his inner turmoil, but couldn't find the words to explain how he felt and besides he didn't want to burden Daniel. Though he briefly told his story of the audition; being bounced into the street and that he'd ruined things with Mari, a woman he now realised must have had a rough time of things with her alcoholic ex-husband.

"Some women are very delicate," said Daniel.

"*Sí*! No *señora* deserves to put up with that kind of nonsense," replied Diego and he began to feel a little better.

He ordered a *café solo* and took a cigarette from Daniel. As he smoked, he gazed across the plaza and thought of *Plaza San Pedro*, back home, and that Saturday was the only day it came to life. *Is that what I really want?* A breeze blew Diego's napkin off the table, and as he reached down to retrieve it he heard the *clip-clop* of a shod horse, like castanets against cobblestones. He lifted his head and, glancing across to the far side of the plaza, he saw a mounted policeman on a white horse, passing a rose-coloured church and turning into a side street. The officer raised the visor of his helmet and glanced over his shoulder. He had a dark beard and his hawk-like eyes met Diego's. Then he was gone.

Diego looked back at Daniel who was waving at a waiter. Daniel turned to Diego and asked, "Something else?"

"*Agua.*"

Daniel placed their order with the waiter.

"Did you just see that mounted cop?" asked Diego.

"When?"

Diego gestured across the plaza. "Just a minute ago, over there."

"By the church of Santiago; no, I didn't see anything. Perhaps he was on his way to another demonstration in the city somewhere? People are still upset after the financial crisis."

"Did you say Santiago?"

"Yes, the Camino path from Madrid to Santiago starts from over there."

It's a sign. Sí, I am still on my Camino, Diego reflected, remembering Leonardo's words about his Camino only just beginning. And the knight and his encouraging words flashed across his mind: "You're prepared to embrace the unknown as you seek out your passions." Diego leaned across the table towards Daniel, shaking with enthusiasm, thinking he'd been lucky to survive the night before; it could've been much worse. He had a second chance. "I was going to return home tomorrow but that would have been a mistake. But I can't stay here either."

"Where will you go?"

"I think I'll know for sure when I get there," said Diego as his hangover began receding. All I know is I've got to keep moving but heading south to *Andalucía* makes sense, into the heart of flamenco. I think somewhere like Seville, where there'll be many touristy *tablaos* and more job opportunities for a guitarist. Big auditions can wait."

Daniel unlatched his guitar case. "You'll be needing this then," he said as he lifted from it Diego's guitar and handed it over to him.

Diego pushed his chair back and sat the guitar upright on his lap. He held it lightly, one hand on its base and the other at the head. The sun gilded its body, and there were no signs of abrasions.

"I didn't damage it?" said Diego, confusedly.

"The neck cracked at the body and I had to replace all the strings, but it survived."

"It's like new!"

"Take a closer look at the rosette."

Diego lowered his head towards the sound hole and saw the words: *La guitarra del Peregrino* engraved around the chain of roses.

Diego felt the letters with his thumb and emotion welled up inside him and he asked, "Did you sleep at all last night?"

"A couple of hours."

"You're a magician."

"No, just a carpenter."

As Diego plucked the strings, the notes vibrated above the hum of the city, strengthening his resolve.

"The best carpenters sharpen their tools in the woods," whispered Daniel.

Diego gave Daniel a quizzical look, but his *amigo* offered him no explanation. Then their drinks arrived. Daniel took a sip from his glass of beer. Diego drank his water and sipped on his coffee, thinking his friend was wiser beyond his years, even though he couldn't fathom out his strange remark.

Daniel bought them a late afternoon lunch and, after they had eaten, Diego realised he should pack his things immediately and start his journey before he found an excuse not to go. Diego stood up and stepped around the table to embrace Daniel, and although he was slender, Daniel felt as solid as a tree trunk in his arms.

"*Gracias* for mending my guitar," said Diego after they had hugged. "Thanks for everything."

"*De nada,*" replied Daniel.

Diego grinned. "Well, I know where to find you should I fall out with my guitar again."

Daniel tipped his hat at Diego and sat back down. He lit a cigarette and gazed across the plaza that was filled with families and people idling about, and he dreamed about the house he would one day own and the workshop he'd build around the back of it.

Within an hour, Diego had returned to the apartment, packed his backpack and written a thank you note to Letizia. He left the note on the dining table, locked up and dropped the keys into her post box at the foot of the stairs.

On the way to the bus station, he cut through Plaza Mayor and spotted Mamadou with his gang selling their wares from outstretched blankets and playing their drums. And, for a moment, he thought about going over to them and busking one more time with Mamadou. But it was time to leave and he knew Mamadou would understand that good memories are often more important than goodbyes. He left the plaza and, tipping the brim of his Stetson over his eyes, he imagined what Seville might be like.

Part II

11

The View from the Bridge

Diego sat at the front of the bus for the view, but by the time it pulled out of the station, his head was resting against the window and he was already asleep. He was dreaming of the cypress tree on the Camino path and its boughs that he'd once climbed. In his dream, he sat astride a thick branch staring across ploughed fields to the horizon. Pilgrims passed underneath unaware of him, though a girl with blonde hair and vibrant eyes glanced up and smiled. The sun descended into the horizon and Diego noticed a campfire casting shadows across the tree. And he saw a ladder leaning against the branch. He climbed down it and his feet landed with a crunch as he jumped from the penultimate rung onto autumn leaves. A tent had been pitched amongst them. Leonardo peeked his head out from within and handed Diego a stick and a piece of bread, and they made toast on the fire. After they had eaten, Leonardo got up, tossed his stick into the fire and disappeared into the surrounding dark forest.

The engine shuddered to a halt and the internal lights of the bus flickered announcing their arrival. Diego woke bleary-eyed, collected up his guitar case and made his way off the bus. Feeling drowsy, he retrieved his pack from the luggage hold and dodged around passengers also making for the exit of the bus station. Outside, he tried to get his bearings. There was a taxi rank in front and he eyed a coat of arms logo on the door of one taxi, depicting a bridge and a temple. He turned around to face the entrance of the bus terminal and above its doors, he saw the sign, *Córdoba* – he'd stepped off the bus too early. Diego dashed back through the terminal to the bus, arriving just as the driver was closing the luggage door. An old couple were slowly climbing the steps onto the bus and Diego waited patiently behind them.

As the couple made their way on board, the image of the bridge on the taxi logo drifted into his mind. He glanced up at the bus and discovered himself turning and walking away from it. Diego crossed the street, passed the taxi rank and headed towards the lights of a tree-lined boulevard. He stopped at a fountain engraved with the words *agua potable*. The gurgling sound of fresh water invited him to take a drink, and as he did so, a dove flapped into the boughs of the plane tree above and a couple of leaves, seared scarlet at their edges, fell into the fountain. A light breeze rustled through the tree, and Diego felt the wind on his right cheek. Instinctively he had found his pilgrim's compass. He thought of the words Daniel had etched on his guitar and he repeated them softly, "The pilgrim's guitar." He tightened his grip on his guitar case and strode forward into the breeze.

The boulevard led Diego to a shopping area and an ornate plaza of bustling restaurant terraces. He glanced around at the tables of diners and promenading tourists, and from somewhere nearby, he heard a serenade of young male voices and mandolin strings. Diego spotted a hole-in-the-wall bar being manned by two older barmen in white cotton shirts, and he went over and ordered a *caña*.

The beer quenched his thirst and he left feeling cheerful, as he followed a pedestrianised thoroughfare downhill. The path opened into a cobbled street and a fortified wall of endless metal-studded Moorish doors, glistening like gold bars in the light of flickering street lanterns. Momentarily, he felt overwhelmed and didn't want to leave this beautiful street. But the path beckoned and led him to a four-pillared gateway, through which, he caught sight of an ancient bridge with numerous arches and the outline of hills beyond. He passed through the gateway and onto the bridge and cast his eyes over the side to a sea-green river. Birds glided close to the water in a V-shape formation. Diego reached into a pocket for his mobile phone and dropped it into the ripples below. It plopped into the water like a pebble and was gone.

Just before he left the bridge, he glanced back, over his shoulder, at a baroque tower. The high walls and rooftops of the adjoining complex blazed ochre as if they'd just swallowed the sun. Diego realised he'd walked by the Mesquita, the historical mosque-cathedral complex. The day was over, but he wasn't ready to stop walking. Still, he paused at a late night tobacconist and bought tobacco, roll-up papers, a lighter, a bottle of water and a bag of crisps. Diego now had less than ten Euros to his name but he didn't mind. He could walk and he could play his guitar. Outside he sipped some water then poured the rest into his flask.

Munching on crisps, he tried his best to keep the moon over his left shoulder and before he knew it he had left the suburbs and the city was below him in the distance. He crossed a concrete bridge over a highway and climbed a gentle hill. The night was clear and he journeyed on for some kilometres along a gravel road, passing through ploughed fields. After a couple of hours, he began to feel tired and looked around for somewhere to bed down for the night.

Diego made out the silhouette of a barn and cut across the fields towards it only to find its double doors locked together by a chain. As he examined them, he spotted the bottom section of one door had corroded away and appeared wide enough to squeeze under. He looked around, noted an owl might be his only witness, removed his backpack and slid his guitar under the door. Diego breathed in and rolled under, pulling his pack behind him.

The barn smelled of diesel and once his eyes adjusted to the semi-darkness, he noticed two tractors and a plough. Diego smiled to himself, thinking of the tractor dealership he'd once worked at, and then he climbed aboard one of the tractors. The seat was made of foam and he stretched out his legs to the foot pedals. He tipped his hat over his nose and was soon fast asleep.

Diego awoke to the creaks of the metal doors being opened and an aroma reminding him of burnt toast. He tilted his hat back and the silhouette of a stocky man wearing a wide-brimmed hat filled his blurry vision. The man secured the open doors and then stopped with surprise upon noticing Diego.

Diego yawned and stretched upright in the seat. All he could think to say was, *"Buen día,"* and in the better light, he made out the man was wearing blue overalls and a straw hat.

The farmer glanced at his backpack and Diego could see although his face was gnarled from the sun, his expression was kind.

"Are you walking the Camino Mozarábe?" asked the farmer.

"Err, no? Mozarábe? Don't you mean, *El Camino Santiago*?"

"Well it's all the same thing," he replied stepping closer to the tractor. "This section is the Mozarábe *camino*."

Diego crept down from the tractor. "*Lo siento*, I didn't mean any trouble. It'd been a long day and I needed somewhere to crash. I saw the hole under the door. I'll be on my way."

"If you'd walked a little further you could have knocked on our door and we'd have given you something to eat. Then depending on your manners, you could have slept in a real bed or the hayloft," said the farmer, grinning a little. "So you're not heading to Cordóba?"

"No, I just came from there. I'm walking to Seville."

"Well, this way goes southeast to Granada. If you jump back on the tractor, I'll take you to meet my wife and she'll give you some breakfast. We'll put you back on track," suggested the farmer reaching out a hand. "*Con mucho gusto*, I'm Paco."

"Diego," he replied, shaking the farmer's hand.

Paco gestured at the tractor and Diego grabbed his things and climbed back up and stood in the space behind the seat. The farmer took his place behind the wheel, and they headed up a track that connected to the road Diego had walked the night before; it arched east into a cloudless sky and through fields, ploughed like ripples in a dark ocean. To the west, the sun's rays mixed with smoke from small fires, burning across fields of raked corn stubbles, creating a magnolia haze and blurring the distant hills. Beyond the hills was the way to Seville.

Paco's house came into view, and he pointed a finger at a yellow arrow of the Camino painted on the back of his gatepost, pointing back up the road. He climbed down and invited Diego inside. Once inside, Diego was greeted by the hisses of a frying pan. They went through to the kitchen and Paco's wife was slicing potatoes into a pan of spicy sausages. Her red apron hugged her rotund figure like a tea cosy.

She looked up from the pan and said, "Paco, we need more eggs." He rolled his eyes at Diego, but acknowledged his wife and left the room. Three cats sat expectantly under the stove and the woman dropped some fried potatoes down to them. "*Buen camino*. Please take a seat," she said, pointing to a wooden table with a spatula.

Diego put his pack and guitar in a corner and drew out a seat. "Sorry to intrude on you like this."

"No, you're most welcome. That husband of mine would have worked in those fields all morning, with nothing more than a piece of bread and coffee in his belly otherwise. He cares more about feeding the pilgrims and migrants that pass by, than eating properly himself. *Gracias*, now he's joining us for breakfast this morning. Well, how's your pilgrimage so far? I always told myself I'd walk to Santiago, but it's so far from here and now my legs aren't so young, not like yours."

"I walked to Santiago a few months ago, but I guess you could say I'm still on a pilgrimage of sorts."

"He says he's walking to Seville!" said Paco, returning with a handful of eggs.

"It'd be easier taking the bus," teased his wife, taking the eggs from her husband.

"You mentioned the Mozarábe, is that what you called it?" asked Diego glancing up at Paco.

"*Sí*," said Paco. "Not so many people walk this section, but it's the pilgrims' way north from here to Santiago."

During breakfast Paco explained that *El Camino Mozarábe* is the most southerly of the Camino de Santiago routes, linking the Mediterranean with the Vía de la Plata route that runs north and connects to the more famous Camino Francés path, which Diego had previously walked. The section of the Mozarábe that Diego had stumbled onto ties the cities of Cordóba and Granada and tracked the historic Ruta del Califato – one of the most travelled routes of the Middle Ages.

"It's waymarked then?" asked Diego.

"Yes, all the way from Almería," replied Paco. "You saw the arrow I pointed out to you?"

Diego leaned an elbow on the table and, mopping his plate with a slice of bread, he wondered if Seville was just a fanciful idea and not the correct path he should be walking. *Granada and Almería are also flamenco places,* he thought. *Didn't Paco de Lucía come from Almería?* And here he was sharing breakfast with another Paco. He chuckled to himself because Paco is a common Spanish name, but he couldn't get the idea of the Camino out of his head, thinking it was trying to steer him back onto its mysterious path and take him somewhere. *Perhaps Almería is that somewhere.* It was a crazy notion, but he remembered what Leonardo had once advised, "Maybe you're on a certain path at the moment whether you like it or not." *So why fight it,* he thought. "How many days to walk to Granada would you say?" asked Diego.

"Around a week or so," answered Paco.

"Don't fancy Seville anymore?" asked the wife.

"I'm not sure."

"*Mucho sol* in Seville," cautioned the wife, gesturing at Diego's guitar case and pack. "You don't want to be tramping around there in August."

"Do you think I'd make a good farmer?" asked Diego, glancing at the farmer.

"No. You've got to like early mornings," said the farmer, smiling as he stood up. "I've much work to do today."

"You can give him a lift across the fields while I clear up here," urged the wife.

"Which direction are you going?" said Paco.

"Towards Granada, and I prefer to walk," responded Diego, getting up from his chair and collecting his things. "*Gracias*. Thank you for everything."

Diego left the house and glanced at the yellow arrow on the post. He looked over his shoulder at the couple and they waved him off and he smiled back. Then Diego turned against the arrow and stepped back onto the Camino, although this time he'd be hiking it in reverse, walking away from Santiago de Compostela and southeast towards the sea. Soon he spotted another arrow painted on the back of a rock, pointing in the direction he'd just come from. He stopped to roll a cigarette and drink some water. And as he looked up into the blue sky he eyed a kestrel hovering further along his path. Diego fished inside his bag, changed into a clean T-shirt and feeling somewhat refreshed, continued walking with renewed hope.

∾

TIMEWORN LOOKOUT TOWERS marked peaks and the path weaved its way through a fortress town, and by the afternoon, the hills were a blanket of olive groves. Diego walked to the beat of imaginary *palmeros'* hands, but his legs were not as well-oiled as they'd been on his original Camino, and he had to stop often. But the tangles of the olive branches provided good shade and, after each break, he was able to march on. A late afternoon breeze helped him further along. As dusk advanced, he arrived in another hilltop town, and he paused at a drinking fountain and filled his flask before he walked up whitewashed lanes to an ancient castle above.

At the top of the hill, Diego strolled around the perimeter of the castle, surveying the land below. The olive plantations encroached on the town like a jungle and easterly blue hills faded into a strawberry haze. He rested in a niche between a wall and a tower and, chewing on a *bocadillo*, a baguette of the breakfast leftovers prepared by the farmer's wife, he watched the sun fade. Diego felt happy that it would rise tomorrow above the hills and light his pathway.

He removed his boots and got into his sleeping bag. And just as he was resting his head upon his guitar case, his eardrums were blasted by what sounded like a foghorn. Diego sat up and realised the disturbance was coming from nearby trumpeting. But no sooner had he pulled on his boots, the trumpeting stopped, and all he could hear was the wind whistling around the castle turrets. Collecting his things, he investigated further around the wall. Beside another towered section, he found the slim figure of a teenage boy with outstretched limbs hopping around the Spanish flag like a bullfighter. On the ground beside him lay a trumpet.

He's a worse matador than he is a trumpeter, Diego thought. But although he observed him with kind amusement, the boy stopped, awkwardly sensing Diego's presence. *"Buenos noches,"* said Diego and nodded at the trumpet. "Do you always come up here to practise?"

The boy half smiled. *"Sí,* it's for the sake of my mother's roof."

Diego grinned and looked up at the sky, "You'd need to make some racket to blow this roof off but I think you got close!"

The boy shrugged, gesturing at the twinkling lights of the town below. "I want to be ready to play in the band for *Semana Santa.*"

"How long have you been playing the trumpet?"

"Three years, but I never seem to make much progress. Though this is my last chance. Next year, after I finish school, I'll be going to seminary."

"Hmm," said Diego thinking. "Do you actually like the trumpet?"

"Eh…"

"…You enjoy playing it?"

"Well, it'd make my mamá happy to see me playing it in the procession behind the cross."

"She's very religious?"

"She lives for Christmas, *Semana Santa* and Sundays."

"I guess it's always been her ambition for you to enrol in the church?"

"Sí señor," replied the boy cautiously. Wondering who he was talking to.

"Funny, my father wasn't a religious man but he once threatened me with seminary when he found out I'd been skipping school. But I always knew it was an idle threat, so I continued bunking off. But I hated him for not carrying through with his threat; it was like he didn't really care about my future. And I was so envious of the *chicos* whose parents had plans for them, who'd already had their futures mapped out. But I wonder how many of them are happy now? What my papá didn't know was I was practising my guitar during those times I was truanting."

The boy sat down on a low wall facing the town below and Diego joined him and they continued talking.

"So you like bullfighting?" asked Diego.

"To be honest, I think it's cruel. But no one could ever tell a matador how to live."

Diego smiled. "Absolutely."

"And what are you doing up here?" asked the boy curiously.

"That's a good question. My mind told me to walk to Seville, but instead I now find my legs walking me to Almería. Guess I'm on a long walk and figuring a few things out. I was just settling in for the night, around the corner, when your trumpeting disturbed me."

"*Lo siento*, but I'm sure Don Quixote and Sancho Panza didn't go to bed early," said the boy smirking.

"Hmm, Don Quixote. I like that, but I'm travelling alone."

"Isn't your guitar, your Panza?"

Diego scratched his head. "Guess it probably is. He never seems to want to leave my side and, believe me, I've put him through hell!" he said laughing. "You like it up here?"

"*Sí*, I like to think of the warrior monks who made it their stronghold. Monks from Calatrava built this castle on the site of an old Moorish fort. They were given charge of defending this area of Spain from the Moors after the Military Order of Calatrava were unable to hold it. Before that, the monks had worked as farmers, shepherds and in manual trades. Can you imagine?"

"*Sí*, I think I can. And the Order of Calatrava, is that similar to the Knights of Santiago?"

"Kind of, they were both religious armies. It's a little complicated, but you could say the Knights of Santiago were a friendlier sort of medieval militia that helped pilgrims. And because of that, they achieved privileges from the Pope and the crown."

"History's your thing then?"

"Some people like memorising football stats, but it's the significant dates and events that mark our history that I find fascinating."

"Are you planning on making a career in the church?"

The boy frowned. "Guess so."

"You're lucky, you still have time," said Diego.

The boy looked at Diego quizzically. "To learn what makes your mamá tick, and for her to understand you. If I had my time with my papá again I'd fight every day to learn about his history and make us understand each other better."

"He died?"

Diego nodded.

"I'm sorry."

"That's okay, but what I'm saying is if you study at the seminary, ultimately it'll be worse for your mother because you'll grow bitter towards her for forcing you down a path that was not of your own choosing." Diego flicked a thumb at the grey smudges of hills in their panorama. "Tomorrow I'll be heading there and I don't really know what lies beyond, but I feel okay about it because it's my choice and I'm learning I can survive by following my own instincts. Can the Bible teach you that? Can the Bible teach you history?"

"It tells us a lot about mankind."

"It's worthy, but it only covers a certain time in history, nothing about the castles and medieval Spain you mentioned," replied Diego running a hand through his hair and thinking. "Not that I paid too much attention, but you know there's so much history along *El Camino de Santiago*, a lot is religious."

"You've walked the Camino de Santiago?"

"*Sí*, and now I seem to be walking one of its paths in reverse."

"The Mozarábe Camino passes through this town towards Cordóba and beyond."

"Indeed it does," said Diego with a smile. "Matador, have you ever considered walking it. I mean, from here all the way to Santiago?"

The boy laughed. "Are you *loco*!"

Diego ignored the boy's laughter and continued talking seriously. "There are remains of pilgrim hospitals, Roman bridges, and of course there's the ancient road itself. And plenty of old churches to pray in, if you wished."

The boy gazed up at the first stars of the night. After a while, Diego broke the silence, "It's a beautiful night. A night to drink a *cerveza*."

"It is," replied the boy quietly. "I could walk to Santiago after I complete my exams next year, and postpone seminary by a year."

"You could."

"Can I invite you to my home, my mamá would welcome a pilgrim for the night. And she has *cervezas*. You could tell her about your Camino."

"She drinks?"

"Only when we have guests."

Diego laughed. "Gracias. A bed and a *cerveza* is a nice offer, but I kind of like it up here. But you'll think about what I said?"

The boy stood up and held the flag above his head. "I will. Wouldn't it be something to carry my flag across this country and plant it in Santiago?"

"It would," replied Diego. "And if you practised the trumpet on the way, by the time you reached Santiago, they might even let you lead an army!"

"Now that would be a miracle," said the boy with a grin.

Diego stood up and, shaking hands, they exchanged their names. The boy's name was Jacobe. He wrapped the flag around his shoulders and Diego watched him disappearing down the steps to the road below. They were very different, and yet, he saw something of himself in him. Jacobe was also a dreamer who had something to offer the world. He just didn't know what that was quite yet.

The wind picked up and, in the final light, he saw the edges of Jacobe's flag flapping. As the wind got under it, the flag filled like a ship's sail. Diego felt hopeful that the boy would cast off the shackles of his mother and live his own adventures.

12

The Olive Señora

Diego awoke to the aroma of baking bread wafting up from the town below. He got himself ready for the day, rolled up his bag up and followed the aroma along dim alleyways to its source, the bakery. He leaned against the stonewall outside, glad for his hot coffee and sweet croissants. The sun was not up yet and there was still a chill in the air. With funds running low, he expected to make several stops that day and busk. He wandered out of the town and found a yellow arrow painted on a wall and he went against it again, continuing to navigate the Camino in reverse.

Diego headed along a boulevard of evergreen trees, at the end of which revealed a Mexican style church, virgin white, against a sapphire sky. The church bells began chiming, a clean polite sound, announcing the hour of seven. After some thought, Diego figured it must be Monday. And he realised how easily he was slipping back into the routine of the Camino, where dates were recalled by significant events and encounters. The bells reached a crescendo, and he stopped outside the church to listen for a moment. The sun made its entrance, warming Diego's face, and he felt glad of it, even though he knew it would soon become much hotter. He better get going.

The path leading away from the church was a steady incline of ochre. Soon Diego noticed the official waymark of the Camino Mozarábe, a rounded stone post, knee-high, with the carvings of a tower, scallop shell and the ubiquitous arrow pointing back towards the church and the town. The marker stated "1114KM to Santiago". Diego began to feel nostalgic about being on another pilgrim path, even though he was walking further and further away from Santiago.

The route passed a park and an abandoned hacienda before it opened out onto a dusty road lined on both sides by olive plantations. It was undulating country, with more distant towers, and within a couple of hours, Diego was hungry again. But the trees didn't part for any settlement, so he soldiered on with faith that the Camino would eventually deliver, as it had always done on the Camino Francés. He thought that before long he'd arrive at a hamlet or roadside eatery swelling with smiling pilgrims. But an hour later he was still walking and he conceded he needed to stop. He rested his back against a timber hut, vibrating with the *putt-putt* of a water pump inside and closed his eyes for a moment. A breeze rustled through the olive trees and he reopened his eyes. Diego smoked two cigarettes, drank some water from his flask and listened contentedly to the sounds of the water sprinklers around the trees. Sometime after, he resumed his journey.

Heat rose in waves along the path and the sun was high. Eventually, the path crossed a stone bridge over a brook, its clear flowing water revealing a colourful bed of red and yellow pebbles, and turned up a steep lane passing a small olive refinery and into a village. Diego stopped at its plaza and looked about. There was a restaurant and a small general shop, though both were as sleepy as the village. He rested on a bench under a tree and searched his backpack for food. Diego found just a few crumbs left in the bag of crisps; nevertheless, he tipped them into his mouth. Then he stepped up to the door of the shop but as suspected it was closed. He remembered he'd seen a drinking fountain on the way to the plaza and decided he should at least fill his flask before he continued.

Off the plaza, a man crossed his path carrying a bag with a stick of bread poking out of the top. Diego assumed he had just been to the local bakery and headed in the direction the man had just come from, but the street soon ended, and Diego found himself looking across to countryside below. He wearily turned about and caught sight of a woman in a crisp white shirt, smart russet trousers and high heeled shoes mopping the tiled steps of her semi-detached house. She looked like she was on a lunch break from the office rather than a housewife. Glad to find someone around, he approached her and shouted, "*Perdón, Señora.*"

The woman looked up with eyes as dark as black olives, shaded by long eyelashes and she studied him guardedly. "Is there a bakery in the *pueblo*?" Diego asked.

He steadied himself on her garden gate, noticing she was very attractive. Diego guessed her to be in her mid-to-late thirties. She was wide-hipped but slim thereafter. Her face was narrow with high cheekbones, and her thick, dark hair was tied behind her shoulders into a ponytail, though a few errant strands curled down her neck. Hands with glossy red fingernails held the mop tightly. After a few seconds, she replied, "It's only open in the mornings."

"Oh," sighed Diego trying to hide his disappointment. The woman resumed her mopping.

Diego followed up with, "*Gracias*," and then he turned to leave.

"Have you been walking all morning?" called out the woman looking back up.

Diego nodded.

"I have some bread. Is wholegrain okay?"

"*Sí*, whatever you have," replied Diego, turning back gratefully and catching the woman going inside her house. She returned with a brown baguette wrapped in paper and handed it across the gate.

"It's not much but the supermarket is out of town."

"It's plenty," said Diego smiling. "*Buenas tardes*."

As he turned to leave again, the woman replied softly, "I'm warming some paella for my lunch, there's lots of it and it needs finishing. Would you like some?"

"Absolutely," replied Diego handing back the bread.

The woman smiled enigmatically, opened the gate and Diego followed her into the house and through to her dining room. She nodded at a round table covered by a spotless tablecloth and went back into the hallway while Diego dropped his packs in a corner then pulled out a chair. In the middle of the table was a kitsch flamenco doll wearing a lavish white dress and green polka dots, and Diego could not help but stare curiously at the doll posing on the tablemat.

The woman returned with a large pan of paella and switched the doll with the pan. Then she left the room with the doll and returned with plates and a jug of iced water and sat down. "Please eat before it goes cold."

Diego ladled a mountain of rice onto his plate and it was only after a series of furious mouthfuls that he realised his behaviour and paused.

"You're hungry?"

"*Lo siento*," he said sheepishly.

"Not at all. It's a compliment to my cooking. Where are my manners? I'm Laura."

Diego put his fork down. "I'm Diego. I'm a guitarist."

They didn't say much more during lunch; Diego was too busy eating, and Laura was happy to oblige and spooned more rice onto his plate - although she did mention she was a secretary at the local olive refinery. Laura had assumed Diego was walking to Santiago, and he didn't dispel that idea, figuring it might confuse if he'd said he was following the path in reverse. After they had eaten, Laura invited Diego into her front room for coffee and he spotted the doll on the windowsill.

Laura left the room to make the coffee and Diego relaxed on the sofa and searched his mind for topics of conversation but it was too arduous against his exhaustion and full belly. He rested his eyes, and within moments he had drifted off into sleep. When he stirred the house was silent and there was a mug of coffee sitting on the side table. He reached for it and took a sip, it was cold and he put it back down. Diego stood up, stretched, and checked around the ground floor for Laura. But the only sign that she'd been there was the lingering smell of the paella. Diego stopped at the foot of the stairs and assumed she must be taking a nap. He called out, "Laura?" but there was no reply.

Diego's foot had already hit the top stair, when he considered leaving a thank you note. But he was drawn along the landing towards the doors. He tapped on the first door and waited for an answer, but it was still silent. He slowly pushed it open and peered in. The shutters were closed, but in the dim light of the room, he could make out two single beds. Diego looked back down the landing and noticed one of the doors on the same side was slightly ajar and he figured it was Laura's bedroom. He tiptoed over to the door and tapped it. There was no response and he peeked inside. The room was also dimly lit but he could see the bed was empty and the sheets were ruffled. On a bedside table was a photo. Diego went over and bent down to take a closer look. Two teenage girls with the same brunette features as Laura smiled out of the frame. He straightened his stance and looked about the room, a chair in the corner was absent of clothes and the doors of the wardrobe were closed. There were no signs that Laura was busy being a Mum.

As he glanced back at the photo, something glinting from under a corner of the pillow caught his eye. He stepped closer and as his eyes adjusted further to the dark, he noticed it was metallic. His hand was already lifting the pillow when he thought he should probably leave the room. It was a handgun. Diego's curious eyes studied it; the body was scratched, and he wondered if perhaps it was a fake or a starter pistol. But as he looked more closely he saw there was a catch to release a magazine. *Who was this woman?* he thought. It was time to leave, right now.

Diego darted downstairs, grabbed his backpack and case and flung open the front door. A crow flew off the gate and brittle footsteps of high heels coming along the street alerted him to Laura returning. She placed a hand on the gate. "You're leaving?" she said squinting at Diego.

"Err, sí. Better get some Ks in," replied Diego cautiously.

"I was going to make you a *bocadillo* to take with you. It'll only take a minute to make, and I wanted to talk to you about something, if I may."

Diego spotted the crow in the upper boughs of a tree. As he wavered, Laura bowed her head and fiddled with a strand of hair. In that moment from the front step, he witnessed a fragile woman full of love. And he allowed himself to lower his guitar case and place it down in the hallway with his pack. Decision made, he responded, "You're very kind."

They went inside through to the kitchen. "Do you like cheese?" asked Laura.

"Anything's fine."

"You're easy to please. And if you want to take a shower, while I prepare your snack, be my guest."

Diego was suddenly aware of his state from the walking and he glanced down at his boots and jeans and noticed they were dusty from the road. Laura opened the fridge, and it crossed Diego's mind that perhaps he was being propositioned and he replied with a grin, "Do I smell that bad?"

"Not too bad," replied Laura grinning and eying the cheese. "I've smelt worse! There aren't many Pilgrim *refugios* on this stretch of the Camino, and my water is hot."

"*Gracias*, I could really do with a shower," Diego discovered himself saying, but instantly wished he hadn't. He had a feeling it would have been easier if he'd just taken her bread and kept on walking.

"You'll find the bathroom upstairs, the door on the left. Help yourself to a clean towel on the shelf."

"On the left, upstairs. Okay," said Diego, feigning ignorance to the layout. He left the room and walked back down the hallway and opened the front door. He noticed long shadows from the fence like the turrets of a castle. He beat off the dust, then sat on the steps and removed his boots. He grimaced from the smell of his own sweat and left the boots on the step. Inside he collected his backpack and cursed to himself on the way to the bathroom.

As he showered, he whispered, "Why do you always do this? You will walk away, Diego. Take the sandwich and go, just be grateful for that." Though he knew he'd likely betray those words and take his chances with Laura.

Diego finished showering and dried himself. Then he pulled all his clothes out of his bag, hoping to find something clean. The best he found was a black T-shirt and his last pair of clean boxers. He put them on, pulled on his jeans and went downstairs to the kitchen. On the side were two *bocadillos* wrapped in foil and Laura was making coffee.

She turned, gesturing at the sandwiches, and asked, "Good shower?"

"I feel like a new man, *gracias*."

"*De nada*. I always take coffee after work to wake myself up for the evening. I could make you one to take away?"

"That would be great."

Laura glanced at Diego's crumpled T-shirt and said, "It's getting late. Alternatively, I could wash your clothes and you could take your coffee here. Or you could even eat with me tonight. Why not make an early start tomorrow? I wanted to ask you about the Camino; it's something I've always wanted to do." She surprised herself at how freely she spoke, even though she knew

Diego was too young and forging his own way in life. But to have a good man in the house, a handsome one at that, just for a night would be something to savour. After that, she wouldn't attempt to delay him any longer. Though she felt a little ashamed about her yearnings, she distracted her blushes by turning to the hob to take the coffee pot off the heat.

"Unbelievably, I am feeling hungry again. And my clothes do need to be washed," replied Diego.

"Hand me your washing," said Laura bending down to the washing machine.

Diego did the talking over coffee. He spoke about his first Camino and his desire to be a professional musician, and how the journey was taking him downstream to southern Andalucía to the birthplace of his idol Paco de Lucía. He admitted it sounded *loco*, but for whatever reason, it now made more sense than anything else. Laura listened intently and Diego's tale continued over a dinner of cured meats, white asparagus salad and red wine. After they ate they retired to the lounge. Laura turned on a lamp and then began to talk.

It was a miracle she was even chatting to Diego she explained as four years ago she'd been diagnosed with a brain tumour and her chances of living had appeared slim. Laura had been forced to give up working and with no other means of supporting her twin teenage daughters, aged sixteen at the time, they took to working and paying the bills. Between them, the girls had held down five part-time jobs and still managed to go to school. They ran the house, nursed their mother and were by her side for her surgery and radiotherapy treatments. And, slowly but surely, the cancerous cells faded and she made a full recovery. Her 'angels' passed their exams and gained good enough grades to go to the university of their choice. They wanted to delay their studies to keep an eye on their mother. However, Laura wouldn't have it and wanted her daughters to go to university at their earliest opportunity.

'Circumstances' had prevented Laura from going to university herself. The previous year she had gone back to work and the twins had left for universities in Madrid and Barcelona. Diego was curious to know about their father and the 'circumstances', but Laura didn't volunteer that part of her story, and he didn't ask.

Not knowing what to say, Diego reached into a pocket and gestured to Laura with his tobacco tin. She nodded in acknowledgement, and he began to roll a cigarette, though just as he handed it to Laura he hesitated. "You smoke?"

Laura smiled. "*Sí*, I know they'll kill you. But that's another form of cancer. After surviving the tumour, I allow myself the odd treat, else what's the point?" She took the cigarette from Diego.

"Well, as long as you think it's okay," said Diego, lighting Laura's cigarette.

Laura took a satisfied drag and then passed the cigarette back to Diego. "We'll share it," she said. Diego smiled and Laura picked up the wine bottle and topped up their glasses. "But maybe, after I've walked to Santiago, I'll give up."

"You will walk it then?"

"*Claro*, you've helped me decide that."

"You could walk it with your daughters? That would be something."

Laura smiled. "Now there's an idea."

"I wish I had your family's determination!"

"Working hard is easy, when you're working towards your aspirations, I learned that from my daughters. Though of course there were times when it was tough, but I was always determined to keep a roof over the three of us." Laura took a sip of her wine, suddenly mindful that she was revealing too much. "You say you're not determined. You reek of determination. Most men only smell of alcohol."

"You don't know me very well," replied Diego taking a puff on the cigarette, before passing it to Laura. He grinned, "But you're right, there was a bit too much of the road on my clothes today."

They both laughed and Laura chinked Diego's glass and her fingers brushed against his knuckles. Momentarily, their eyes locked. Laura suddenly returned the cigarette, collected the wine bottle and stood up.

"I hope you don't mind, but you'll have to sleep on the sofa. I don't like anyone sleeping in the girls' room."

"Err, *sí*, I understand. That's fine," stuttered Diego. "The sofa will be luxury compared to where I slept last night. I have a sleeping bag."

"I hung it on the line with the clothes to air. I'll fetch you some bedding."

"Okay, *gracias*."

Diego glugged his wine and handed Laura his glass before she left the room. He stubbed out the cigarette and looked about the room trying to work out how he felt.

A few minutes later, Laura returned with a bundle of bedding, but she hovered for a moment, then said, "It's been a long time since I've shared my bed with anyone else but the girls. If I were to invite you into my bed, would you just sleep next to me, nothing more? Just two people sharing a large bed; I would like to know if that's what I want again."

Diego saw the image of the gun under her pillow but he wasn't nervous; her request was sincere. *For whatever reason*, he thought, *she fears someone*. He replied, "Okay, I can do that."

He followed Laura up the stairs and he went into the bathroom. Diego stood still with the light off; moonlight blurred through the frosted window, etching the bath and sink. And he had the image of Laura bathing two young children. He turned the light on, peed, washed and took a deep breath.

A shard of light led Diego across the hallway and into Laura's bedroom. She was tucked in the far side of her bed, facing away from the door. He removed his jeans, dropped them on the floor and got into the bed. Laura reached out a hand and turned off the bedside lamp. Diego cautiously turned away from Laura to face the door. He didn't feel any bumps under his pillow but he couldn't sleep. Laura was also restless. If Diego had have touched her, she would not have refused him, but she also respected him for sticking to the deal. And she began to feel frustrated with herself for not telling this good man all of her story. Perhaps the wine was also having an effect on her; she wasn't quite sure. So a few minutes later, sensing Diego was still awake, she placed some fingers on the back of his head. Laura needed to be honest with him before he left. "You have thick hair, like a horse's mane," she said and sat up. Laura switched on the lamp and continued talking.

When she was little more than a teenager, she had got together with an older man who ran his family's successful grape farm. He was charismatic and popular, especially as many locals were employed on his farm. They married within a year of meeting and he was supportive about Laura's plans to study for her degree in Granada, even though she would soon be a mother.

Then out of the blue, a disease swept across the grapes in the region, blighting the season's crop. Laura's husband borrowed heavily to keep the business going, but the land didn't recover in time to keep up with the repayments and the bank foreclosed on the business and auctioned off the land. Her husband felt humiliated and sought solace in drink. He was an angry drunk, and many times violently took out his pain on Laura. Then, one night, he came home paralytic and threatened to burn down their house with them all in it. When he left the house and stumbled around in their shed looking for diesel, Laura bolted the front door and gathered her babies along with some money that she had stashed away. Her husband was banging on the front door threatening to burn them alive, while Laura left with her children through the back door and drove off to a new town and life. He burnt the house down before doing the same to the local branch of the bank that had foreclosed on the grape farm. He husband served a prison sentence of ten years and, ever since his release, Laura feared he might one day show up.

"You've never seen him since?"

"The last time I saw him was in court. He wrote but I never read his letters."

"What about your family, are they…"

"It's just me and my angels," interjected Laura.

"Now is your time. You have to walk the Camino and then you must study," offered Diego.

"I will," replied Laura.

"*Gracias* for sharing your story with me."

"*Gracias* for listening."

Laura slid down into the bed. "Do you mind if we sleep now, I feel exhausted?"

Diego yawned. "*Sí*, let's get some sleep."

Laura switched off the lamp and their backs brushed together as they turned over. Diego wanted to hold Laura, though he didn't want her to get the wrong impression and he wasn't sure he could trust his lustful desires. So he let her be and he thought of Laura as one of the many beautiful flowers on the Camino that had stopped him in his tracks. Though he'd been tempted to pick some, he never had.

DIEGO AWOKE EARLY and slid quietly out of the bed, leaving Laura sleeping. He picked up his jeans from the floor and went into the bathroom. He peed at length and felt strong. Then he took a shower. After he went downstairs to the kitchen and was met by Laura in her dressing gown brewing coffee.

"I promised you takeaway coffee," she said with a smile.

"You're first on the list if I'm ever looking for a wife," said Diego with a grin.

Laura laughed. "You'll soon forget about me."

"I don't think so," said Diego and he found himself blushing. "Err, did you see where I left my hat?"

"In the dining room with your guitar."

Diego collected his things and Laura retrieved Diego's clothes and sleeping bag from her backyard. They met back in the kitchen and Diego changed out of his T-shirt and into his fresh denim shirt while Laura poured Diego's coffee into a polystyrene cup.

"I can make you some breakfast," said Laura.

"You've already done too much for me and, as you'll find out, there's nothing better than eating along the Camino."

"I look forward to experiencing it," said Laura, handing Diego the *bocadillos* that she had made the evening before.

Then they hugged and, although they both felt a spark again, the allure of their own individual roads kept the embrace brief. Seconds later, Diego had collected his load, left the house and was waving goodbye to Laura. He walked towards the plaza, thinking he could pick up his path from there. En route he stopped at the fountain and sat down on the edge of its stonewall. Next, he removed the lid of his coffee and unwrapped one of the *bocadillos*.

The sun was just breaking above the houses, and he eyed his stretched shadow on the street as he munched his *bocadillo*. Two cyclists with scallop shells tied to their panniers shot down the hill at the end of the street. The men spotted Diego, waved and shouted, "*Buen camino.*" Diego returned the same pilgrim greeting and when the echoes faded he heard the distant hum of a tractor.

This is really living, he mused as he finished his breakfast and dipped his flask into the fountain. Then he headed up the hill and out of the village to a quiet highway. Diego crossed the road at a gap in the barrier over to a Camino marker, almost hidden in the undergrowth, pointing down to the village he had come from. He glanced over his shoulder and felt he was leaving a mystical place concealed among the groves; only revealing itself to pilgrims or those in need of sanctuary. Canopies of trees hung over the trail, beckoning Diego. He needed no other encouragement, adjusted his hat and followed the path deep into the wood.

13

Bandits

Diego's feet sprang along a trail of dried pine needles. The only sound was the occasional rustle of the wind through the trees. The path led gently downhill and soon he was absorbed in his thoughts.

Like Mari's bed, Laura's had felt good. But already Diego was starting to forget about Mari, and he figured it wouldn't be long before Laura was also just another faded footprint in his trail. *Why do I always treat them like that? Good señoras who deserve the best from men.* He looked along the dappled path, searching for an answer, then a passing breeze lifted the tops of the pines, and they sighed and cast shadows on the trunk of a holm oak. And he caught a glimpse of a place at the margins of his memory; the twisted shadowy fingers of a witch's hand dancing along his bedroom wall, cast there by the old oak tree outside his window during a thunder storm. He had felt safe in that *madriguera*, the rabbit's burrow, made for him when his mamá was alive. She'd always sat on the edge of his bed and stayed there until he was asleep and the storm had passed. Though after she passed away, he became afraid of storms again, even through to adulthood.

He stopped and rested his guitar case against the belly of the holm oak and stretched his arms around it as his eyes welled with tears. He finally understood. In those other women's beds he'd always been looking for that warm safe place he had known as a child.

After a minute, Diego relaxed and sat against the tree. He stretched out his legs, drank some water and almost immediately began to feel better. He looked back at the Camino, then towards his own path and a tunnel of overhanging trees.

The trail soon opened into a raked landscape, which made for pleasant walking. Diego shared a smoke with a man beating almonds from a tree, and not long after he was munching on a bunch of grapes gifted to him from a woman who ran after him from her allotment. A Roman road led Diego over a small stone bridge and he spotted in the distance another fort with high walls shrouded by olive groves. He arrived at the outskirts of the town, where the everyday sound of dominoes being slammed onto a table filtered out from a bar, tempting him in to spend the remains of his money. Elderly men sat around a table playing the game, seemingly unaware of Diego, while a group of farmers sat at the bar drinking a variety of spirits. He dropped his luggage at the counter, rested a boot on the metal footrest, ordered a *caña* and drunk in the scene.

It was all very familiar. The banging fists of the domino players; the younger men who waltzed in to buy cigarettes; the middle-aged barmaid humming as she filled the tapas cabinet with sardines, Spanish *tortilla*, cheeses and the typical fare. The necks of the farmers at the bar, twisting like wooden corkscrews, either up towards the television screen or down at their newspapers. And occasionally a mother would drop in to buy some sweets for her child and a lottery ticket for her dreams. The weather entered their conversations; it was always *"mucho calor"*. But Diego didn't need reminding it was too hot; he knew it full well.

There was a calmness to their lives and, like Papá, these townsfolk would probably live their whole lives in the town, Diego surmised. And it made him think again of his Mamá, and how, for some, death comes prematurely. *Yet, there will always be death. We can't hide away from it*, he found himself thinking. And he wondered if that was why many cling to familiarity – as if somehow, they could prevent danger and death from entering their *madrigueras*. He wasn't sure he was any different.

He finished his beer and eyed the tapas cabinet. Checking his pocket, he felt some change, and ordered a *tortilla* from the barmaid. But as he gestured to pay, the woman dismissed his hand and stated matter-of-factly that pilgrims do not pay in her establishment. Diego felt humbled and realised it was her way of acknowledging those who had the courage to face the uncertainties of the road ahead. He left the bar, grateful for his visit.

Diego spotted a Camino arrow painted on the curb, pointing away from the town and the hill he needed to climb. It wasn't long before he arrived in the main plaza. It was exposed to the sun, but a cool breeze whistled through the awnings of the surrounding cafés, shops and around the statue of a dignified man, whose inscription had faded with the passage of time. Diego sat on a bench beside the statue and hungrily ate the remaining *bocadillo* and *tortilla*. It seemed like an age since he'd last played, but as he counted back the days he realised it was no more than four, and yet Madrid already seemed a lifetime away. He grimaced thinking about his penultimate day there, but in the same moment, his mouth twisted into a smile, as he thought about the good *amigo* he'd made in Daniel. Diego removed his guitar from the case and ran his fingers over the etchings around the rosette, and it made him feel good to know that Daniel believed in his journey. The wind picked up and ruffled his hair. Although it was still very hot, the breeze reminded him that autumn was probably no more than a month away.

The town was peaceful; Diego figured people were eating lunch, though he was happy to tune the guitar and play to himself as he rested on the bench. But with the taste of coffee and tobacco on his mind, he eventually stood up, hopeful of some passing trade. He placed the open case by his feet and dropped his remaining change into its crimson interior. It was quiet and, just as he was about to call it a day, a young-looking man, with dark curly hair hanging down to his shoulders, came out of a nearby bar and placed a five Euro note into the case. Diego acknowledged his generosity with a spirited *picado*, then brought his sparkling middle fingers to a swift halt, brushing the strings deliberately with his thumb.

The man gestured to Diego to take a seat at a table outside his bar. "Let me buy you a coffee."

"*Gracias*, you read my mind," replied Diego as he gathered his things and joined the man beside the table.

"I was going mad in there – it's a slow day and your music has lifted my spirits."

The man went back inside the bar as Diego sat down at the table and rolled a cigarette. He smoked, watching the smoke buffeting around in the breeze, and when the barman returned with his coffee, Diego asked him where everyone was.

The barman wiped the table, gave the plaza a cursory look and then sat down to join him. "Mostly old people here now," he said.

"What brought you here then, you're from Italy, no?"

"My accent is always a giveaway." He grinned. "The usual brought me here."

"Ah," Diego smiled knowingly. "Where did you meet her?"

"In London."

"She's from here though?"

The Italian nodded. "This is her family's bar, and we're managing it for the summer. The problem is all the younger people who used to come here went to London to work in its bars and cafés."

Diego laughed. "Figures, right."

The Italian smiled. "Love is blind as they say." The Italian glanced at Diego's guitar case. "Are you playing somewhere locally?"

"No, just passing through."

"You're walking the Camino then?"

Diego hesitated before he replied. "Kind of, in reverse."

"So you're walking home now, after completing it?"

"I have walked to Santiago, but that was from my home in Castilla y León."

"Ah, I see you're a free spirit. Busking's good in Granada from what I've seen."

"*Bueno*," replied Diego with a smile as the Italian continued talking.

"It also made me a free spirit. I walked to Santiago a few years ago when the company I worked for in Italy went bust. Ever since I've been working in different countries." He glanced up at Diego's Stetson. "But perhaps I'd describe you as a gaucho."

Diego laughed. "I've never been on a horse in my life."

"*Claro*," said the Italian smiling. "But that's a great hat you're wearing."

"And what about you; how do you see yourself?" asked Diego.

His expression turned serious, "I'm Italian. Need I say more?"

"No, not really," said Diego as he smiled. "I briefly worked for an Italian. Italians seem to know their place in the world."

"*Sí*, home is something that's inside you; home is who you are."

He's right, Diego acknowledged to himself. *I am a guitarist*. He knew that magic feeling of *Inori*, would always be with him, wherever he played. He could remember his village, he could remember Santiago, he might even recollect this bar, but there was no need to hold onto them. The journey was everything.

After a moment, Diego asked, "Do you have a map of the area?"

"You don't have a phone with a mapping app?"

"I got rid of it, thought that would be a smarter move."

"I understand, I remember seeing one pilgrim on my Camino with his head down at his phone, ignoring an arrow and heading straight for a stack of hay – it was hilarious."

They laughed and then the Italian remembered that inside the bar there was a copy of a Camino guide. He nipped back inside, returned with a booklet and handed it to Diego. It was from the Almería – Granada Jacobean association.

"Can I make you another coffee?" asked the Italian, noticing Diego's cup was empty.

"You're very generous, but I can't take another one for free."

"Don't worry. Pilgrims drink for free on my shift."

Over his second coffee, Diego studied the booklet and its maps, which suggested there were some two days of walking left to reach Granada, and after that, around a week to reach Almería. There were also a scattering of *refugios* on the way to Granada, though no cheap accommodation options in the current town, Alcalá Real, just a couple of *pensiones* and hotels.

Diego finished his coffee and went inside the bar. It was empty apart from an elderly couple eating in one corner. The Italian was drying some glasses as Diego stepped up to the bar and placed the booklet down on it.

"*Gracias* for the coffees and the loan of the map," said Diego. "Time to hit the road again."

"*Buen camino*," replied the Italian reaching out a hand across the bar.

They shook hands firmly and Diego replied, "*Igualmente.*"

Diego turned to leave. The Italian put his bar towel over his shoulder and eyed him as he stepped back into the street. *How easy it would be*, he supposed, *to just step from behind the bar and journey with the guitarist*. But he resumed drying the glasses, knowing he and his girlfriend would soon be working in a new place and meeting more people. He just didn't know yet where that might be.

Diego walked towards the statue, looking around for a yellow arrow to contradict. After a minute he hadn't spotted one and looked across to the main street, running downhill. It felt like the natural way, and he walked down the hill.

At the bottom, Diego noticed a signpost marking the Ruta del Califato, and followed a track that led across open fields leading to hilltop villages. Streaks of clouds like handfuls of pink candyfloss lit his evening's path as he climbed a steep gravel track into another village. He slumped into a corner of the only bar in the village and, after refuelling on two *cañas* and the tapas that came with them, he decided to climb to the very top of the village to its castle. The blanket of night had already draped across the village by the time he passed the citadel's first crumbling wall and the portico of a church invited Diego to roll out his sleeping bag and burrow in for the night. The church bells rang on the hour, every hour, but Diego slept peacefully through their chimes.

He awoke with the dawn of day, sat up in his sleeping bag and stretched out his arms. Pulling off the bag, Diego put on his boots and climbed the last stretch of the hill to the castle. When he reached its crumbling walls, he stood back to admire the panorama. The sky was bleached by the early light of the day and clouds resembling snowy mountain peaks were suspended in an otherworldly manner, above smears of a real mountain range. He was viewing the Sierra Nevada. And in the valley below, brushstroke smudges of buildings twinkled in the first rays of the sun.

Diego eyed the view with wonder, it felt as if Granada was waiting for him. He stood there for a few minutes before gathering his things and leaving the village with renewed vigour. A wide path running close to the road led him to another village a few kilometres later. The remains of his money bought him a coffee and bread and jam in a bar already dusted with sugar sachets and till receipts.

A brisk morning's hike took him to a cobbled road bridge crossing a fast-running brook. A whitewashed stone arch straddled the far side of the bridge into the town and, as Diego walked through it, to his surprise, in a niche there was an icon of the Virgin Mary. A car sped through the arch and the driver, a man with the look of a gypsy, made the sign of the cross and eyed Diego with a sly look. The high revving of a motorbike followed, rattling the closed shutters of shops. Diego looked around and across from the bridge to see a male teenager tearing up and down the street on a small Japanese motorbike. It was custom painted with orange flames, and the teenager was pulling wheelies to impress a small gathering of youths.

Diego stepped away from the icon and took a couple of paces back. The town looked gritty and intimidating. But he was hungry and he needed to try his luck busking. *Trust*, Diego asserted. *What's there to be nervous about?* Tightening his grip on his belongings he tentatively crossed the bridge, bowed his head and turned up the hill. He heard the squealing of the engine first, before the biker pulled alongside him, reached out, and yanked at his guitar case. Diego instinctively gripped the handle more tightly and tried to pull it in. He yelled, "What the hell! It's mine." But the power of the bike was too much for Diego and the biker pulled the guitar out of his grip.

"¡Ay!" the biker whooped as he glanced back over his shoulder before throttling up the hill. The sun dazzled

Diego's eyes as the motorbike and his swinging case disappeared into its haze.

"*Puta,*" was the first word that came to mind. Diego screamed the word with the passion of a gypsy lament. He stamped and looked about. The youths had scattered and the gurgles of the brook below were the only sounds. *Thieving gitanos,* he thought. And he stood in the middle of the street like a stunned rabbit; then after a minute he lurched over to a low wall above the brook and sat down. He caught his breath, gripping the straps of his backpack in disbelief. After a while he glanced down at the water and back up to the arch across the bridge. His attention was drawn to a weather vane on top of it. The arrow pointed back through the arch and uphill to the other side of the town, and hovering high above it was a kestrel. *A sign?* It was all he had to go on, so he got back up and strode over the bridge and up the hill; rage growing with each step.

Graffiti sprawled peeling whitewashed walls and cars were parked haphazardly in a maze of concrete streets. The sounds from televisions inside the walls of box-shaped houses gave Diego the feeling people were peering at him from behind their curtained doorways. At a junction of alleyways, he came across two men sitting on plastic chairs outside a house with a flat corrugated iron roof. Their sharp goatees and sideburns resembled pieces of felt loosely stuck onto their red bloated faces. He noticed one of the men was missing some front teeth and the other wore gold knuckle-duster style rings. Diego resiliently said, "*Hola,*" as he walked by. They didn't respond, though he felt their eyes burning a hole in the back of his hat as he continued climbing.

Further up there was a local pharmacy on the other side of the street and Diego crossed over and paused in its shade and looked about. Any hope of retrieving his guitar felt as redundant as the town. *What kind of person would rob a man of his guitar?* he thought. But he couldn't give up trying to find it. "Would Papá? No," he whispered. *If someone had stolen his candyfloss cart, he would have staggered on with his mad eyes and stubbornness until he'd got it back.*

Diego felt incredibly thirsty and reached into his pack for his flask but, as soon as he opened it, he remembered he'd finished the last of his water earlier in the day. He wiped his sweating face with a shirt cuff and scanned the street for a fountain, but all he saw were breezeblocks, dust and more graffiti. He wanted to rest but he pushed on until there were no more box houses, just cave like dwellings. The residences had been tunnelled into the undulating hillside and they resembled giant molehills with small chimneys. Arriving at the final cave, a dwelling with a makeshift porch constructed with a piece of plastic protruding over its door, he spotted the same custom-painted motorbike parked next to a scooter. Diego walked over to the door. He felt like rushing in like a bull, but he took a deep breath and managed to rein in his anger. *He's not going anywhere*, he thought. Subsequently, he noticed a few metres down the street a wall shading some steps leading down to a dirt football pitch. Diego went over and sat on a step and leaned behind the corner of the wall. Tipping the brim of his hat over his eyes, he rolled a cigarette and waited.

Diego was on to his second cigarette when he spotted the thief swaggering out of the house gripping his guitar case. He wore cut-off jeans, revealing gangly legs and white sports shoes. And he was smirking all the way to the edges of his narrow jawline. Though he was tall, Diego figured he was no more than sixteen years of age. He stubbed out his cigarette, slid down a couple of steps and waited for him to pass by. Seconds later, the thief passed him unnoticed. Diego sprang.

At the sound of Diego's boots scuffing the concrete, the thief darted like a deer into a side street. He stealthily weaved past obstacles, and Diego kept him in his sights as he chased him down. The thief flicked his head over his shoulder and frowned with surprise that he still hadn't shaken off Diego. Next, he jerked into an alley that led to a wider street but Diego stayed on his tail. The street opened into a shaded plaza with a small single-storey school. Diego caught up with him at the perimeter railings and rugby tackled him to the ground. The guitar case fell to the floor with a bounce.

Diego squatted on top of the thief, pinning his knees hard into his shoulders. His eyes hardened and he raised a fist. The thief looked expectantly up at him and his eyes were dark, like deep wells; and staring into these liquid pools Diego suddenly felt an immense sense of pity for the teenager and his wrath was gone. As Diego wavered and tensed his legs to stand up, he felt a sharp cramp in them and he was forced to kneel. Sweat was pouring off him and he felt faint. His head drooped and his body swayed. He placed a hand on the ground to steady himself, before he passed out.

WHEN DIEGO STIRRED, he felt the sheen of a soft cushion under his head. His feet came into focus at the end of the sofa he was lying on. The room was murky but strips of light fell on him from a porthole style window. At the corner of the window was an alcove carved into the plaster and earth, and his backpack, guitar case and hat had been placed within it. Diego tilted his head towards the light. A man with a dark mullet hairstyle, tanned face and a horseshoe moustache was standing over him. He handed Diego a glass of water.

Diego held the glass and took a sip. Then he started to drink uncontrollably.

The man raised a hand and said with a husky voice, "Tranquilo."

Diego paused and looked curiously up at him.

"Drink slowly *amigo*. We brought you here to my house after you passed out. My nephew was the one who took your guitar."

Diego took a sip from the glass and recalled the earlier episode. He coughed and asked, "Your nephew?"

"*Sí*, and I apologise on behalf of our family. He should know better and he will be punished. To pinch a wanderer's guitar is to take away the scythe of a peasant." The man felt one end of his moustache and Diego noticed thick wrinkles in the joints of his fingers and his nails were those of a guitarist. "And a lone guitarist should know better; never walk in the afternoon sun in this heat, let alone go chasing after a *gitano*!"

Diego glanced at his guitar case. "As long as it's not damaged, there's no harm done."

"Your guitar is okay, I checked it myself. But you should not forgive so lightly," replied the man as he cocked his head towards the window and a doorway. "Luka get in here and explain yourself to our guest," he yelled. He looked back, "And our guest is…"

"Diego."

Luka arrived at the doorway and stood hesitantly by the window, looking at the floor.

"All of a sudden you have nothing to say? Over here, now and apologise to Diego!"

Luka cautiously stepped over to the sofa and his uncle clipped him on the back of the head and said, "Well?"

"*Lo siento*," Luka mumbled as he looked up and again Diego saw pain in the teenager's eyes.

Diego sat up, took another sip of his water and glanced at his case again. "It's okay, it's been returned to me now." He forced a smile through cracking lips. "And you've shown me I need to take it easy in this heat."

Luka replied with a slight nod.

"Are you walking to Granada?" asked the uncle.

"*Sí Señor*."

"Well, you will be our guest tonight and, tomorrow morning, if you get up at sunrise, you'll be in Granada before it's too hot. And call me Pachego, everyone does." He then squinted at Luka.

"Tonight this nephew of mine will be your personal gofer. Okay, I need to spread the word that we're hosting a little fiesta. Rest up and prepare yourself, Diego."

Pachego clipped Luka around the head again and they both left the room. A minute later, Luka returned with a bowl of stew and gestured for Diego to eat. Then on his way out, he closed the shutters of the window and Diego ate the broth slowly in the dark. And after eating, he fell asleep.

~

THE BRIGHT SOUNDS of flamenco guitars roused Diego hours later. Opening his eyes, Diego took a deep breath and breathed in the night. He sat up and reached for his glass of water from the floor and took a sip. Light flickered through the gaps in the shutters. Diego stepped onto the floor tiles, crept over to the window and peeked through the slats of one shutter. Hundreds of candles lit a small gathering of people sitting in a semicircle around two seated flamenco guitarists, one of whom was Pachego. The guitarists' hidden eyes and closed-mouthed smiles revealed a portico to a world Diego was becoming more familiar with, that of *Inori*.

Diego listened for a minute before he put down the glass, found his boots and headed to the bathroom to freshen up. Then he went outside to join the party. An old woman in a black dress took hold of Diego's arm, led him over to Luka and indicated he should sit beside him. Luka was clapping his hands in time to the music, but broke rhythm and gestured with a hand the ubiquitous sign of a *cerveza*. Diego nodded and sat down on the spare seat. Luka got up and walked over to a large dustbin filled with icy water and bottles of beer. He returned and cracked the lid off the bottle with his teeth and handed it to Diego, before losing himself to the music again. Next, the old woman handed Diego some more stew. Heads in the gathering nodded at him and he nodded back and ran a hand through his hair a little awkwardly.

The guitarists' lyrics contained more blood, forbidden loves and persecutions than Diego ever thought possible to fit into a single song. And they were dusted with words of different dialects or part phrases. '*Andaluz*', and he figured '*bajañi*', meant guitar and they sang '*¡Ay de Mi!*', the song of the last Moor. Often they would repeat the same song or *palo*, yet the lyrics were never quite the same. At times their tones echoed the squeals of a catfight or squawking seagulls. *Their flamenco is different*, Diego thought. It was unconditional. And as the night progressed and he clapped and stamped his feet some more, he began to feel more connected to the gathering; like he was one of the many flickering candles.

Throughout the night, Luka continued to bring Diego food and beer but at the point when he thought his belly couldn't take it anymore he raised a hand and said stop. By then the fiesta had died down to its embers but two women still burned brightly, as they danced along a table. Diego glanced at them, but he broke away from their charms as he felt Luka's eyes on him.

"Are you good?" asked Luka.

"You mean as a guitarist?"

Luka nodded.

"I get by. And do you play?"

Luka fiddled with a studded earring in his left ear as he thought about the question. Then Pachego joined them.

"Diego, your hand is empty, has Luka not been keeping you watered?"

Luka glanced at his uncle with searching eyes. Suddenly Diego understood why he had snatched the guitar: he had done it to impress his uncle; he was desperate for his approval.

"He has, too well! I'm starting to feel drunk," replied Diego. "You're a fine guitarist."

"*Gracias*," said Pachego.

"And what do you do when you're not playing the guitar?" asked Diego.

"I'm a businessman."

"What kind of business?"

"Import and export," answered Pachego abruptly.

Diego glanced at Luka and asked, "A family business?"

"It's a skilled business. It's very subtle; not everyone can learn or should try to learn it," replied Pachego, dropping his voice to a whisper and rubbing his wrinkled fingers.

Diego began to realise that the family business was likely an illicit one.

"Could you strum us something?" said Pachego, changing the subject.

"Better you hear me play when I've had less to drink. I'm learning that the guitar and booze is a bad mix for me," replied Diego. He glanced at Luka. "But do you play?"

"His father did but not this one," exclaimed Pachego.

Luka's eyes dropped.

"That's a shame," said Diego. "It usually runs in the family, from my experience."

"Maybe; but not everyone has the discipline to learn," declared Pachego, cutting Luka a sharp look.

"Hmm," said Diego under his breath and he turned to Luka. "You've never played?"

"A bit, a few chords when I get the chance. But that's not often," said Luka a little glumly.

"*Amigo*, you've had less to drink than me. How about we add some more chords to your repertoire. What do you think?"

"I'm thirsty," bemoaned Pachego, before he turned and headed back to the remnants of the fiesta.

Luka took a fleeting look at his uncle and noticed he was distracted in conversation again. Then Luka eyed Diego and nodded.

STEPHEN R. MARRIOTT

"I'll get my guitar," responded Diego.

Diego went inside and fetched his guitar, and when he returned, Luka was sitting on his own. Diego pulled out a chair and pushed the guitar into Luka's lap. Luka looked silently down at the guitar and Diego pressed some fingers of Luka's left hand along the neck of the guitar. But Luka pulled his hand away.

"I'm left-handed," he mumbled.

"Oh!" said Diego. "Let me think about that a minute."

Diego took back the guitar and flipped it the other way, so its strings were upside down.

"It's not a problem, you just have to remember the lowest notes are now at the bottom," he said strumming the strings with his left hand.

Diego then demonstrated a chord and then he repeated the process with some more complicated ones. Next, he gestured to Luka to try for himself and passed him back the guitar.

Luka hesitated but he sensed Diego's will urging him to play. He gripped the guitar and pulled it into his belly. And edged his right hand along its frets, brushed the strings with his left hand and then he played the chords. Soon he added a couple he hadn't been shown. Diego stood up and asked, "What's your story?"

"What do you mean?"

"With you and your uncle."

"You noticed?"

"Who wouldn't? He seems, well…" Diego gathered his thoughts. "He treats you like the black sheep."

"He's okay really. He's been like that since my father passed away."

Diego nodded sombrely and Luka continued. "My father was the older brother and the head of the family and the business – or as we say, he was the *jefe*. But we fell out with a rival family. The dispute was bad for business on both sides; then one day my father went to see the family; to try and resolve things. But he got into a fight with some men in their family and they killed him. Since then things have been erratic and my uncle, the new *jefe*, tries to control everything, thinking he can hold it all together. And he won't trust anyone to do anything. But he doesn't understand I am no longer a boy, and it's my family too."

"Well, you're very much your own *hombre*, especially with the guitar," said Diego. "And I'm sorry about your father."

"That's okay, I've got used to him not being around. He taught me some stuff on the guitar, but he struggled to teach a left-hander."

"Let me show you some more then," said Diego as he reached for the guitar and sat next to Luka.

Luka mimicked the melodies that Diego showed him and, within an hour, Luka's eyes were shining and Pachego had been drawn back by his nephew's growing repertoire of songs. He watched on with curiosity at a master and apprentice working in complete dedication to each other. Eventually, Diego looked up at Pachego and said, "He's finding his own style."

"*Sí*," said Pachego in his husky tone. Subsequently, he turned to the dancers on the table and clapped his hands loudly. They were moving around the heads of some men who'd passed out across the table. Pachego cried, "Drunken *gitanos* time to go! Our maestro needs his sleep – tomorrow he's walking to Granada."

Luka looked up at his uncle and he responded with an approving nod. Luka handed Diego his guitar and said, "*Gracias*."

Diego winked and said, "And thank you for returning it without a fight this time."

Luka smiled and gestured towards the house. "Let's go in and I'll get you a blanket."

Diego surveyed the scene; half the candles were still flickering and the sky was a pale blue lampshade. "I've been sleeping half the day, and it won't be long before the sun comes up. Think I'll make an early start. Can you fetch me my things?"

"You feel okay now?"

"I'm good, and I want to walk off the alcohol."

Luka went into the house and when he returned Diego and Pachego were shaking hands.

"Perhaps I'll pass by again someday and take a guitar lesson from you?" said Diego as he released his grip.

Pachego half-smiled and said, "I'm a busy man, but come back anytime."

Diego put his hat on and heaved his pack onto his shoulders. Then he tipped his hat at them and went on his way.

14

Granada

Diego climbed a bridge over a railway line. From the bridge he viewed the foothills of the Sierra Nevada, just visible in the early light on the hazy horizon. A farmers' access road on the other side of the bridge, trailing alongside the railway line, would be his way into Granada. A train thundered by and he marched on in its wake. Three hours later, just after seven, his shadow stretched into Granada's suburbs and soon after he was striding along an elegant boulevard, passing by statues of former idols of the city. Diego tipped his hat at one of them – a serious-faced female flamenco singer.

The boulevard led him to the historical centre and past the tall arches of the city's cathedral, and into souk-like alleyways, lined with rows of touristy shops. In one of the alleys, he spotted an ornate tile on the wall and painted with the Camino arrow with the inscription: *Camino Mozarábe*. Soon after he found himself in a large deserted plaza, surrounded by shops and grand apartment blocks, its only occupant was a dog curled up beside a stone fountain. Diego felt the urge to continue across the plaza and up a cobbled incline, leading to the promenade: Paseo De Los Tristes.

Diego looked up around him and his attention was grabbed by a fortified structure on a nearby hill, which loomed down over the city. Its stone blocks were glowing in golden light as the rising sun appeared from behind the main tower as if being released from within its walls. The Alhambra palace was famous, but Diego had only ever seen it on television and in print. Its alluring presence brought him to an immediate halt.

As he gazed, Diego felt the cool air of the late August morning on his cheeks and he had a flashback to home. *If Papá was still alive*, he reflected, *we'd be having breakfast about this time now*. Late August had been the one time of the year when Diego had been up early for his seasonal work, harvesting the wine grapes. Normally he rose too late to share breakfast with the old man. On those August mornings, his father had never been grumpy with him. Papá would ask about the progress of the harvest, always asking if Diego's crates had weighed more than those of Ricardo's and Javier's.

There had been something special about stepping into the silent fields with the thin mist wrapping around the vines. During the harvest, much of the village was involved and, at the end of each long hot day, there was often a communal dinner on the plaza outside Bar Paradiso. And there was always plenty of wine, but somehow Diego had managed to temper his thirst during those evenings. Getting up the next morning with a fresh head and doing his bit had always seemed more important. Though, after several weeks of nipping his fingers and suffering from an aching back, he was always glad when it was over. But what he didn't know then, but now understood, was that he was resourceful and capable of making money in other ways.

Diego felt grateful for that insight. He turned his head and strolled over to a wall, where below ran a fast-flowing stream. No doubt his present view of the Alhambra was something Papá would have enjoyed hearing about also. Relaxing Diego dropped his baggage against the wall and sat down on it. With his back to the Alhambra, he rolled a cigarette. As he smoked, he observed the space ahead of him; considering where the best evening busking patch might be. Yet he couldn't postpone it until then, he was again starving. However, he waited patiently until he spotted a waiter setting out tables under the awnings of one of the restaurants that lined the promenade. Diego slid off the wall and approached the waiter, suggesting he could play some songs in exchange for breakfast.

A man with shaggy long hair and a bushy beard, wearing a bright tie-dyed T-shirt looked up from a corner table and waved at the waiter.

"Double up on the hummus and seat this musician at my table," he said abruptly.

The waiter pulled Diego out a chair and Diego joined the man. Sitting down he noticed behind the man's chair a bulging laundry bag.

"*Gracias*," said Diego.

"You need a room?" asked the man.

Diego leaned back in his chair and eyed the man curiously. "I've only just arrived. I haven't planned that far ahead."

"Mariachi, don't take too long to make up your mind – good rooms go quickly."

"Is the room here above your restaurant?"

The man smiled. "So you thought this was my restaurant. No, it's not my business. I live in the Albaicín."

"The Albaicín?"

"Hmm. Don't they teach you anything about your country in your schools? It's the old Arab quarter. The best *barrio* in town."

"*Gracias* for enlightening me," responded Diego, mildly sarcastically.

"You won't find a cheaper room in the Albaicín."

"Okay, let me think about it. But *perdón*, I need to freshen up. I was travelling through the night."

The man nodded and Diego got up and went inside the restaurant to the bathroom. After he'd relieved himself and was washing his hands, he glanced at the mirror above the sink and noticed his beard was back. He cupped some water into his hands and splashed it on his face. Droplets clung to his bristles and suddenly he felt the need to shave, take a shower and rest up for a few days. And though the man buying him breakfast appeared the irritable type, he was a little intrigued by him.

Diego returned to their table now laden with hummus, bread and a French coffee press. The man gestured to Diego to eat, and he responded by spooning some hummus onto his plate. The man reacted with a shake of his head and raised a hand.

"Watch," he said seriously. He picked up a piece of bread, cupped it in his hand and mopped it around the bowl of the hummus before he scooped the creamy paste into his mouth.

"It's lousy hummus, but there's no excuse not to eat it properly," he said after swallowing his mouthful.

Diego followed suit and they resumed their breakfast, though the man continued to berate the food; mentioning Spanish bread was no substitute for Jewish bread before exclaiming that all the best food came from Israel. And if Diego doubted it he should look it up in the bible. Diego didn't get much of an opportunity to speak, but he seized the moment when they'd finished eating and the man's attention was diverted to rolling a cigarette. He confirmed he'd take the room for just a few days, but he could only pay for it once he'd earned some busking money. The man grumbled a little but nodded and then told him his name was Nadav. Diego responded by reaching out his hand. "Diego," he said as they shook hands.

They talked some more as they smoked and drank their coffee. Nadav revealed he always took breakfast at this restaurant before setting up his artisan pitch. Hearing that, Diego insisted he'd give him a hand. And though Nadav protested, stating he had his own system, Diego stuck his heels in and responded, "The charity of food should always be repaid with a good deed. Look it up in the bible," he exclaimed, doing his best to keep a straight face.

After breakfast they walked over to the wall Diego had been sitting on and from the laundry bag, Nadav removed a lavender coloured silk sheet. They spread it out over the ground, weighing the edges down with pebbles. Nadav mentioned the pebbles were from the stream below and that some older *señoras* still collected stones from it during *Semana Santa*, and then when a storm headed towards the city, they'd hurl the stones from their windows in its direction, hoping the sacred stones would ward off the evil spirits of the storm.

"Come on!" responded Diego. "Maybe in some remote villages they might still do that but not in this city."

"You'd be surprised; I've seen plenty of strange things amongst you Spanish since I've lived here."

"And how long's that?"

"Too long *amigo*!" replied Nadav before he changed the subject and went into his bag and pulled out a handful of bangles and necklaces.

Next, he went into great detail about how to position his merchandise correctly across the sheet. Afterwards, he asked Diego to pass him some tubes from the bag; and he unrolled some paintings and placed them delicately across the cloth, weighing them down with more pebbles. Then he stood back to admire his makeshift stall.

Diego grinned. "With those mystic pebbles holding down your paintings down, there's no chance of a storm blowing them away."

"Hmm, something's not right," said Nadav doing his best to ignore Diego. He squatted down and reorganised some of the paintings.

As Nadav rearranged them, Diego took a closer look. Their brushstrokes swirled with new age symbolism and abstract shapes. And though the pictures captured the earthy colours of the city, they didn't do much for him.

Parasols were now popping up at the other restaurants and people were on their way to work, but they had yet to draw much custom.

"Why so early?" asked Diego.

"If you knew how hot the Granada sun gets, you wouldn't have asked that question!" responded Nadav, fidgeting and nodding up at the sun, which was now high above the towers of the Alhambra. "It's always a race to beat it before it becomes unbearable."

"But…"

"You have some smokes?" interrupted Nadav.

"*Sí*," said Diego, figuring he'd find a better time to offer his ideas. He dug a hand into a pocket, found his tobacco and proceeded to roll Nadav a cigarette.

They sat on the wall above their pitch, and Diego passed Nadav his cigarette, then made himself one. After a while, Diego asked Nadav what had brought him to Granada.

Nadav took a long drag on his cigarette, and then launched into his story. "I ended up here after my extension in the IDF ended."

"IDF?"

"Israel Defence Forces. Not long after I was conscripted, I was promoted to an officer. I proved to be a good one, and when my mandatory service was drawing to an end, I was asked to serve a further year. The post was to help with the withdrawal of Jewish settlers from the Gaza strip. Back then I believed in the threat from Palestine and felt it was an honour to be asked and to continue to serve my country."

"What changed your mind?" Diego asked, sensing there was more to this story.

"They turned me into a Roman Centurion," he declared describing a standoff with the IDF and their bulldozers and distraught families, who didn't want to leave their homes. During that confrontation, he became disillusioned with the conflict, figuring borders were just lines in the sand, drawn up by bureaucrats and politicians.

"I was one of the last Israeli officers to leave Gaza. Then it was just a wasteland of rubble. When I left, I wanted to get as far away from the conflict as possible. I bought an old Citroën Estate with my final stipend."

"And that's how you ended up here?"

"Well, I drove north through Syria and Turkey, before heading west along the Mediterranean coastline, but as I headed up through Spain, my car broke down in

Granada. It was as good a place as any to decamp for a while.

"My thoughts exactly," commented Diego.

"But almost ten years later I'm still here. I never expected it to be for so long."

"I discovered I could get by in Granada, doing my thing." Though Nadav conceded the competition on the streets was now much stiffer, with many more hawkers and migrants passing through the city. And that was one of the reasons he had tried to make some sales in the daytime, whilst the competition was hiding away from the sun indoors.

Nadav paused and relit his cigarette. Diego wiped his forehead with the cuff of his shirt as he digested the story. After a moment of silence he asked, "What about your family, they're in Israel?"

Nadav stood up from the wall and crouched down to rearrange his products, ignoring Diego's question. To his relief, a tourist ambled by and took a casual interest in the wares.

THROUGHOUT THE MORNING, they did little business. And when another customer took a fleeting look at the paintings then walked away without buying, Nadav started collecting together the merchandise. "Help me with this; it's too damn hot to make many sales today."

As they packed up, Nadav talked enthusiastically about the lunch he would make them, and the thought of food raised his spirits.

Walking up the steep lanes of the Albaicín to Nadav's apartment, Diego glanced at Moorish doors leading through to grand houses and wondered who'd once lived behind them. *Had it been rich sultans or Jews, but never gypsies*, he supposed. They passed through a stone arch shaped like a large keyhole. Nadav mentioned it was a former gate to the city.

When they reached Nadav's apartment, he asked Diego to remove his boots and socks, and to his delight, the tiled hallway felt like fresh snow against his baking feet. Nadav tidied away his merchandise into a built-in cupboard in the corridor, where Diego noticed his paints organised on a shelf. They went into the kitchen-diner, which had a small wooden table and two wooden chairs in the centre of the room. At the far end, sunlight poured in through a gleaming window. The only other furniture was another wooden chair beside the window. A pile of books was stacked neatly on the floor by the chair. Nadav went over to the window, pulled across the shutters and turned on the light. Next, he went over to the stove and began preparing their lunch. Diego removed his hat and within a few minutes, Nadav was placing a pan of poached eggs nestled in a broth of spicy tomatoes in the middle of the table. Diego mopped up the dish with homemade flatbread and Nadav announced they were eating shakshouka.

After they'd eaten, Nadav filled the kettle and left the room. He returned moments later with a shell-shaped stringed instrument, with a long fretted neck, and he held it up proudly.

"Well, it's definitely not a banjo," said Diego.

"It's a bouzouki!"

"Ah, *claro*, how could I have forgotten?" replied Diego with a grin.

"They come from Greece."

"Is it just Greeks that can play them?" said Diego winking.

"No, I play. But let me make the tea first." Nadav placed the instrument on the table and went over to the stove.

After preparing the tea, he sat back at the table and Diego said, "It won't play itself."

Nadav looked back nervously. Diego took a sip of his tea. Nadav cautiously took hold of the instrument and drew it towards his chest. He'd been trying his best to master the bouzouki and he needed to ask a musician if he was wasting his time. Nadav hadn't needed to hear Diego play to know he was in the presence of a great guitarist – Diego had walked self-assuredly with his guitar and not once had he bragged about his music.

As Nadav plucked some strings, Diego took another sip of tea and sat back in his chair to listen. Nadav began strumming and as his runs on the strings picked up, the sharp tones of the bouzouki fascinated Diego's ear, blending together familiar sounds of both Greek and Arabic music. Diego sensed stories emerging from his instrument. Occasionally, Nadav missed a note and cursed but Diego gestured him to continue. After a couple of songs, Nadav took a breather and placed his bouzouki on the table and drank his tea. Then he glanced at Diego with wide eyes, inviting him into his world of vulnerability.

"Love it, very cool! But why did you stop," said Diego smiling. "It was just getting interesting."

"Really?"

"Seriously, and you've given me an idea. I have a proposal for you."

Nadav's eyes narrowed. "If it's a business proposal I warn you, Israelis are very shrewd."

Diego grinned. "In that case, I better be on my game. Would you mind if you show me the room; I didn't get much sleep yesterday. A shower and a nap would surely aid my skills of negotiation."

"I have never understood your siesta custom," replied Nadav standing up. "You need a towel?"

"That would be great."

Nadav grumbled something under his breath but nonetheless left the room to fetch Diego a towel. When he returned, he showed Diego to his bedroom and the bathroom.

DIEGO AWOKE TO the melodies of the bouzouki. He stretched and sat on the edge of the single bed as he absorbed the stories of the bouzouki's strings. They spoke of Arabian caravans and long desert crossings intersected by high sand dune mountains, carved by the *siroco* wind that blew across the Sahara and into Spain. Diego felt his smooth shaved face, collected his clothes from a chair in the corner by a low window and dressed. He opened the shutter and peeked out the window. The alley twisted thinly downhill and the balconies of the houses and apartments on either side practically touched. Diego withdrew his head and went into the kitchen.

Nadav stopped playing. "Good mattress, no?"

"I slept like a log," replied Diego as he reached for his hat and put it on.

"Heading out?"

"We both are, I hope."

Nadav's bushy eyebrows rose towards thin wrinkles on his forehead.

"I need to make some money fast to pay you and continue my journey south to Almería." He took a breath. "Nadav, you have nice things to sell, but you need to get them in front of more customers."

"Street trading is different to busking!"

"Maybe, but I think we can combine their best aspects."

"Diego, how do you propose we do that?"

"Trust me," said Diego, adjusting his hat. "Where's the busiest plaza in the evenings?"

"That would be Plaza San Nicolás – it has the best view of the Alhambra during sunset."

"Well, we'll pitch up there then."

"It's not available."

"Not available?"

"It's *La Mafia's* spot."

"What do you mean?"

"The local gypsies won't let anyone else perform there."

"They play flamenco?"

"*Claro*, well rumbas mostly."

Diego grinned. "That's okay; we'll just play anything but rumbas."

"We?" said Nadav agitatedly.

"*Sí*, you on the bouzouki, me on the guitar."

"That's not my thing. I trade in the streets. I don't perform," said Nadav standing up, before disappearing out of the room with his bouzouki in hand. He returned moments later without the instrument. "Besides, I trade in the day."

Diego sighed. "Okay, how about I play the guitar and let's see if it can draw a crowd, and you take care of the merchandising?"

Nadav thought for a moment and then said, "What would be your take?"

"Twenty-five percent of any sales you make while I'm performing?"

"Hmm," muttered Nadav as he tied his hair back with an elastic band and considered the offer. Twenty-five percent would eat heftily into his profits, but he wasn't too worried as he thought they'd only be making a small number of sales "Okay we try it for one night, but it won't work and we'll have a poor spot in the plaza."

"Let's find out," said Diego, reaching out his hand.

Nadav reluctantly shook Diego's hand and soon after they left the apartment.

THEY ARRIVED AT the far side of the plaza beside a gift shop, putting a café terrace and the tall bell tower of a white church in between themselves and *La Mafia* who busked with an unfettered view of the Alhambra. Tourists gathered beside them admiring the pink hue of the Sierra Nevada and the sand-coloured blush of the palace.

Nadav nodded towards the gypsies. "Listen, they're playing a rumba!"

Diego glanced in their direction but he didn't pay too much attention, and went about securing a piece of cord between a lemon tree and a lamppost and then took out a handful of clothes pegs from a pocket. He showed one to Nadav, who grumbled but followed Diego in hanging out his pictures across the improvised line. Below the dangling paintings, they placed the silk sheet and arranged the necklaces and bangles across it. Afterwards, Nadav stepped back to admire their display, which was lit from the light of the lamp. He didn't say anything and instead concentrated on rolling a cigarette.

"Keep your eyes open for the cops," said Nadav after making the cigarette.

"We'll be fine, we have a whole view of the plaza. Though we'd better start before it gets too dark."

"Okay."

Diego took out his guitar, drew it close and closed his eyes. He discovered it was his gypsy favourites he felt compelled to play, but now there was a more playful swagger to them. Nadav looked up from where he was sat with his trinkets, his glum mood had vanished and he eyed Diego with admiration. Soon the sun bowed out and Diego's music draped around the silhouetted figures of *La Mafia* and their tourist audience like party bunting. Suddenly the tourists found Diego's music and the merchandise and Nadav found himself busy making sales.

As Diego wound down from a song, he spotted the gypsy musicians huddled together. One of them, a man with a dark complexion, and a razor-sharp jawline running down from his leather Stetson was sharing out their busking takings, though he kept a scrutinising eye on Diego. Diego met his look and the gypsy reacted by fingering the brim of his hat and subtly bending it. The man nodded at the other gypsies and they went on their way.

With half of Nadav's stock sold and the crowd beginning to dwindle, they called it a night at that spot. As they were packing up, the proprietor from the gift shop came out and enthusiastically introduced himself and proposed that they regularly set up stall and play outside his premises. He explained his end of the plaza never got much passing trade, but that evening his shop had experienced its best day in years. In return, he could offer them a commission on any sales he made during their time outside the shop. Nadav struck a deal with the shopkeeper and Diego suggested they move on and try their luck along Paseo De Los Tristes. Nadav hesitated at the idea, as he considered he might sell out of stock and that would create a temporary problem. But he snapped out of his concerns as he observed Diego eagerly gathering up the merchandise.

They chased down through the Albaicín and, in less than quarter of an hour, they had arrived at the promenade and were setting up in a quiet corner next to a gallery away from the swarm of other hawkers and buskers. They tied the cord between two conveniently placed pomegranate trees that were blossoming with orange flowers. Soon Diego's music glided around the plaza. He was like the pied piper, and people flocked over to them and the gallery.

It wasn't long before the gallery owner came out and befriended them both. She was an Oriental lady with a gentle face. She mentioned that twenty years ago she'd fallen in love with Granada when visiting on holiday and never returned to her home country, Singapore. She captured the city on her canvases and sold them in her shop. And, like the previous shopkeeper, she'd magically found her sales lifted that evening. Nadav didn't waste any time and quickly struck a commission deal with her. Though this time he upped the rate. And Diego and Nadav promised to return outside her shop the next evening. They were both exhausted, but very happy with the bundle of cash they had made that night. It was close to eleven and they decided to call it quits for the day.

15

El Siroco

It had been another long and hot evening, and it had just gone midnight. Diego and Nadav rested around the kitchen table cooling down in the breeze of a fan mounted on the kitchen work surface. Nadav took a drag on his joint and offered it to Diego, but he reacted with a casual shake of his head.

Diego got up to make tea and, while he was waiting for the kettle to boil, he made some calculations in his head. It'd been his best ever two weeks of street earnings. Just then, an idea struck him; he poured their teas, sat back down and, removing his tobacco from a pocket said, "Nadav your handicrafts are selling well and the commissions are good, but do you think there's a way to do even better?"

Nadav flicked some ash into an empty pizza box and raised his eyebrows. "Diego, I know I can be on a downer sometimes, but really I'm happy with how things are going. Why change anything?"

"*Sí*, but I'm not going to be here forever. I think you have the potential to charge more money for your paintings."

"It's too late for this conversation," sighed Nadav.

"Just hear me out. Have you ever painted people before?" said Diego, making himself a cigarette.

"That's not my thing," snapped Nadav. "You don't like my paintings?"

"There's nothing wrong with them, but every evening we see all those fascinating people on the streets. And in their faces, we learn something about them. How about sharing that in your art?"

"Do you know how long it would take to paint them? It would be years before we had enough pictures to sell."

Diego lit his cigarette. "But you know what I mean?"

"*Sí*, I've seen it."

Nadav took a long drag on the remains of his joint and then stubbed it out into the box. Then, he took a sip of tea and said thoughtfully, "I always wondered what it'd be like to be a good photographer."

"Photographic portraits. ¡*Estupendo!* They would really sell."

"When I was in Gaza, I saw the war photographers going in and out; there were some good ones – they took risks. But I don't think many of them saw what you see when you're stationed there long enough. After a time, the dust settles and you see in people's eyes all their hopes and fears. I'd have liked to have captured their faces in photographs."

"Well here's your chance to do it in Granada."

"Good cameras are expensive!"

"You can afford it now. I know I've got enough money to sleep and eat well all the way to Almería. Think of it as an investment." Diego leaned across the table. "And don't you want to get your car repaired? You could go home; after all, you said you never planned on staying here long term."

Nadav rolled himself another joint and he thought about home. He could hardly blame Diego for assuming he wanted to go back. In one way or another, he was always making intimations about Israel. But could he really go back after all this time and start over? Nadav thought about it and wondered what he would do. He had got used to living his simple life in the Albaicín, and his spare room had always sublet well, which supplemented his income. But, deep down, he'd known for a long time that Granada wasn't his place.

"Why not give photography a go?" asked Diego.

"What if I'm not any good at it?"

"You're an artist. Once you said you couldn't even play a note on the bouzouki and each time you practice you progress, no?"

"Hmm," muttered Nadav as he lit his joint. "Everyone thinks they're a photographer these days." He exhaled slowly. "And what is it with you and Almería?"

"Almería?"

"*Sí*, your obsession with getting there. The city has even been finding its way into your songs lately."

Diego explained it was the birthplace of his flamenco hero, Paco de Lucía, so it was a pilgrimage of sort. He felt that seeing his statue and finding guitar work there would be the inspiration he needed to keep believing and progressing. Adding that the Camino was guiding him there; it was transpiring into his destiny.

Nadav leaned back in his chair and began laughing. Diego had never seen him laugh so hard before. Nadav tilted his head back as he laughed and the wrinkles on his forehead widened like the husk around a ripened almond. Diego wasn't sure if he was being mocked but he wanted Nadav to stop.

Eventually, Nadav caught sight of Diego's stony face and he wiped his watery eyes. "*Amigo, lo siento*. It's just that you won't find any statue of Paco de Lucía in Almería."

"What do you mean?"

"He was born in Algeciras, further along the coast," answered Nadav, doing his best to hold a straight face.

"I was sure he was born in Almería," said Diego with quiet humiliation.

"No, definitely Algeciras. I stopped there on my journey here. I saw his statue and I remember thinking it'd be a cool place to have lived. Algeciras is on the Straight of Gibraltar, across the bay from the Pillars of Hercules. The Pillars are the rock of Gibraltar, which looks towards Jebel Musa, the mountains in Morocco, which are visible from that point in Spain. Legend says Hercules split the mountains that once joined Africa to Europe, creating the Straight of Gibraltar, hence the Pillars are the remnants of the unifying land bridge."

"Oh," said Diego.

"Don't worry though, just take a right when you hit the coast at Almería and keep walking for, say, some five hundred kilometres," said Nadav, as a grin split his regained composure.

"You seem to know a lot."

"There's a lot of time for reading in the army."

"What do I do now?" said Diego.

Diego stared motionlessly at the fan. The whirring sound blocked out all the noises of the city. There was no drunken merriment in the streets below, no church bells, no distant fireworks. Not even a lovers' tiff from one of the nearby apartments.

Nadav looked at his friend with concern. All the earnestness he'd witnessed in Diego throughout their short time together had suddenly vanished in a puff. "Okay, I'll buy a camera. And let's see if we can make some more money selling street photography prints to our customers, Diego."

Diego continued to look blankly at the fan and drank his tea silently. After a few minutes, he put his mug on the table, stood up and said, "I'm going to bed now. Tomorrow we can look for a camera, and with the extra money we make, I'll have enough funds to return home and to buy back my papá's candyfloss cart."

∼

THE NEXT MORNING they found a camera shop in the old Jewish quarter. It had everything from old cameras to the most modern digital ones. Nadav insisted on buying a second-hand 35mm film camera, which he bargained hard on. Diego didn't attempt to interfere, even though he thought digital would be a much faster route to production of the prints they could sell. His thoughts were occupied with the business of candyfloss selling. And, he figured, why stop at his papá's old pitch? He could also set up other carts in more villages and expand the business. Then perhaps he'd be too busy to think about his pilgrimage and the guitarist he could have become. And if he couldn't forget, he could always imagine and play the odd gig at Bar Paradiso or sometimes further afield in Burgos. He told himself that he should be happy with that; after all, his papá had settled for much less.

Nadav managed to negotiate some free rolls of black and white film, and after making the purchases, Diego left him to roam the streets with his new camera. With much of the day to himself, Diego suddenly felt at a loss with what to do with it. He spotted some people boarding the tourist bus for the Alhambra, and as it rattled by, he decided it was time that he also visited the palace.

It wasn't a long walk but perspiration dripped off Diego's nose as he ascended a shadeless road. Arriving outside the palace's main entrance, he was met with bus loads of tourists and an endless queue. He nearly turned around but first, he filled his hat with water from an ornate fountain and drank from it. Then he placed the hat on his head, and he felt good as the last of the water cascaded down his face. He noticed finches now bathing in the fountain, dipping their red bills into the basin and flicking the water around their heads. Diego wiped the water from his brow with his shirt cuff and joined the line of people. To his surprise, it moved quickly and before long he had passed through the palace gates and was strolling through lush gardens and was being drawn to a view of the city. San Nicolás's church glowed brightly in the sun and red rooftops merged with dark swelling hills and he realised he was looking north at the land that had led him to Granada. Hundreds of kilometres beyond was his village. To the west, the foothills of the Sierra Nevada faded into an azure horizon and, somewhere behind them, Diego supposed was the sea.

He wandered along red fortified walls, past commanding towers and under reconstructed arches. Although the grandeur and scale of the complex was lost on him as his confused mind tried to make sense of his journey. *Could I walk a further five hundred kilometres to Algeciras?* he asked himself. And he felt angry for being wrong about the birthplace of his music idol. But Algeciras had never appeared on his Camino radar. Diego began to question why he hadn't given Madrid more time. The Alhambra felt like a labyrinth, and suddenly he wanted to leave.

At that moment he found himself in a courtyard of Moorish arches and windows, casting silver paths of light across the tiled walkways. Diego went over and followed the tiles into a high ceilinged hall. The wooden beams of the hall resembled the hull of a galleon, and star-shaped domes floated above adjoining rooms. In another room, he overheard a tour guide explaining that the area had once been the throne room, in which King Ferdinand and Queen Isabella had granted royal backing to Christopher Columbus to discover the New World. She mentioned Isabella had sent for Columbus, while he was crossing an arched bridge containing a tiny chapel of the Virgin in a village just north of Granada, called Pinos Puente. Diego's attention was captured immediately and he continued listening. He learned that Columbus had been on his way to France, downtrodden, having given up hope that the Monarchs would support his dream. But with the news, he'd turned his horse around in the middle of that bridge, and headed straight back to Granada with the Royal messenger. Whether it had "been divine intervention, or not," she added, "we'll never know but as they say the rest is history."

Diego stepped outside of the old throne room and sat down on a shaded bench next to a beautiful green pool. Its surface was as still as a millpond and captured dark shadows of the arches of the throne room. He reflected on his observations and the words of the tour guide. *People make their own history, as long as they believe. I should just commit to my journey*. But then another other voice in his head told him to wise up. He may have crossed the same bridge as Columbus, in Pinos Puente, but that didn't mean anything. Besides, the Paco he'd met after Córdoba was a farmer, not some kind of messenger or apparition of Paco de Lucía, and there was nothing waiting for him in Almería, apart from washed up dreams. And it would be *loco* to walk all the way to Algeciras.

He got up, left the palace and headed for the Albaicín. On his way, he passed a *tablao*, and glancing at its door, he saw a poster of a *señorita* curling with one hand the hem of her crimson flamenco dress above her head, like she was summoning a large swell in the ocean. His eyes cut back to the street and, disheartened, he carried on; thinking he could hide away in his room until the evening.

Stepping up his pace, he soon arrived back at the apartment and went in. Diego entered the kitchen and something brushed across his hat. He looked up and, hanging across the room, were many strips of film negatives. Nadav came in behind him, holding a dripping strip of film. Smiling as he clipped it to one of the lines with a clothes peg.

"I see you like your new camera then!" said Diego.

"I had a bit of a stroll around with it."

Diego examined the pictures on one strip. Then he went about the others looking at them in fascination.

"What do you think?" asked Nadav cautiously.

"They're *excepcional*," replied Diego, turning to Nadav. "Really! It's proper art." He paused. "I mean not that your paintings aren't art."

"Diego it's okay, I understand."

In the negatives, Diego had seen market stallholders, migrant hawkers, street cleaners, gypsies. They were in their everyday environments, but captured in Nadav's lens, somehow their ordinariness had gone. There was no subjectivity and, in their intimate gestures, there was acceptance of who they were – it was *Inori*.

"This is your thing," said Diego. "It has to be shared, how do we get the prints made?"

"I don't know. I had shadowy memories of developing negatives in an art class at school, and I Googled what I couldn't remember. I haven't looked into making the actual prints yet."

"Did you turn the bathroom into a darkroom?"

"*Sí*, if you need to piss be careful and don't turn on the light!" cautioned Nadav.

"Don't worry," replied Diego with a wry smile. "Perhaps the negatives can be printed digitally?"

"I did see a scanner and a sign about printing photos at the photography place."

"Well the negatives will dry in no time, let's get them down there and we can start selling them tonight," replied Diego, rubbing his hands.

Nadav began to grumble, stating it might be expensive. But Diego was already taking down the dry negatives and he didn't give Nadav time to dwell on his doubts.

A WEEK HAD passed, and Nadav's photos were selling well. They had fixed large black and white prints to their improvised line in the streets, where the old paintings had hung. The Singaporean gallery owner had also taken a liking to them, and framed the photos and displayed them on the walls of her shop.

Nadav worked hard in the morning taking photos, then developing them and Diego managed the printing of the negatives at the photography shop. And he was enjoying his time working with Nadav, especially as his grumpiness had almost gone. However, he'd told himself that it was now or never if he was to set up the candyfloss business. He made up his mind that the next day he would leave for sure.

"You're on your own tonight," said Diego, just as Nadav was gathering the merchandise together that evening. "I want to see some flamenco before I go home tomorrow."

"You have enough money now?"

"More than enough."

"But who's going to sort out the prints? I thought we were partners."

"Come on you already do all the hard work – you could even invest in your own scanner now. You don't need me anymore."

"But what about your music? No one will come to the stall now."

"Your photography is a big enough draw."

"But we entertain. It's all part of it!"

"Wait there," replied Diego leaving the room.

Moments later, Diego returned holding Nadav's bouzouki. "Here's your entertainment."

"No, I'm not good…"

"…Stop saying that," interrupted Diego as he held out the instrument.

"You're definitely not joining me tonight?"

"No, I'm going to head up to the flamenco caves."

"Those shows are just for tourists."

"I know, but I want to see one for myself before I leave."

Nadav frowned, but Diego stubbornly pushed the bouzouki towards him.

"Okay, but don't get ripped off," replied Nadav, reluctantly taking the bouzouki.

Diego left the apartment and strolled up a hill, past the whitewashed walls and into the gypsy quarter of Sacromonte. He followed a single-laned street, which wound around a steep gorge and the river below, before opening into a wide thoroughfare, where the soft rock of the hill had been carved out into underground grottoes. Once gypsy families had lived in these cave homes, but now they were used as venues for flamenco shows. A couple of performers idled about outside one of the caves smoking and gossiping. Diego nodded at them and peered through the entrance of the cave and into a warren of tourists cramped together on narrow tables. Waitresses threaded around the tables with carafes of wine, topping up the tourists' glasses.

A male gypsy singer stepped down from the stage and danced among the tables, and to Diego's surprise, the singer could also dance. Never before had he seen a flamenco singer also dance flamenco. His footwork soon became flashes of stamping heels and, as they echoed around the cave, the tourists yelled, "*Olé, Olé!*" raising their glasses at the performer, but also gesturing for more wine. Diego wondered whether the gypsy's talents were really appreciated by the drunk tourists. He'd probably do the same thing for another coach load of tourists tomorrow. Diego stepped back into the street, feeling wretched. And he didn't understand why – was this man's performance for the ignorant tourists not confirmation enough that he was making the right decision to return home. During his time in Granada he hadn't felt the urge for anything stronger than tea, but suddenly Diego felt extremely agitated and he felt the need to drink a beer.

Diego desperately looked around for a bar. Built into the side of the hill and on the first turn of a winding lane, he spotted a *taberna* terrace with plastic tables overlooking the flamenco caves. Diego drifted up the hill to be greeted by an old man sitting inside the entrance. His demeanour was melancholic and his face was wrinkled like a roasted pepper bell, contrasting vividly with his freshly ironed, white linen suit. He raised a quivering finger and pointed Diego to an empty table overlooking the flamenco caves. Diego glanced at the other empty tables, but figured it was as good a table as any. The landlord disappeared inside the bar, also chiselled into the hill, and reading Diego's mind returned with a bottle of *Alhambra* beer. He feigned a smile and placed the beer in front of Diego. Before returning to his seat.

Diego glanced back at the landlord, figuring that making small talk might help lift the man's gloom but then a cat jumped onto the man's lap stealing his attention. So instead Diego took a swig of his beer and stared out across the gorge at the omnipresent Alhambra. It was floodlit and appeared like a bright beacon against the encroaching dark velvet of the night.

He drank his beer quickly and went inside the bar to find the toilet. In the urgency to find it, with his mind distracted, he didn't spot the flamenco memorabilia dotted around the walls. The bathroom was little more than a broom cupboard and, in its dim light, he listened to his urine pounding the toilet with the intensity of the dance steps he'd heard earlier. For a moment, Diego had the feeling he was standing in the snug toilet at Bar Paradiso and the thought struck him that he must have pissed more than a thousand beers and Euros into its toilet in recent years.

He washed his hands in a small basin and, feeling a little flushed, he splashed some cold water on his face. When he stepped out of the room, he paused to catch his breath. As he did, he spotted a Spanish guitar attached to the wall behind the bar, as well as framed photos of flamenco dancers and musicians on the other walls.

Diego returned to the terrace and caught the landlord's attention. "Is it still possible to find traditional flamenco in this *barrio*?"

"My neighbour used to be a flamenco singer, now all my neighbours are bohemian hippies," replied the landlord wistfully.

"That's a crying shame," said Diego, keeping a straight face as he thought of Nadav, who could pass as a hippy. After a moment he said, "But I noticed you had a decent looking guitar hanging above your bar?"

The landlord put the cat down and looked up at Diego. "You play, son?"

"*Sí Señor.*"

"My guitar hasn't been played in years. Shall we see if there's any life left in it?"

"Why not?" replied Diego.

The landlord stood up slowly and, with a sweep of his hand, gestured across the empty terrace. "After all, you aren't going to chase anybody off!"

He went inside, then returned with the guitar and handed it to Diego. Its cherry-coloured body had faded over the years, though its edges glistened in the warm glow of the terrace.

"It's light," remarked Diego.

"It's made of Indian rosewood, the best material for any soloist."

Rosewood was Paco de Lucía's material of choice Diego recalled as he replied, "*Sí*, it's the best."

"Well, let's see what you've got."

Diego pulled out a chair and sat down. He plucked a string and the note was as toneless as lead clanging bells. The tuning pegs were made of wood, and Diego fiddled with them and, eventually, the guitar's tones became richer and its lower notes were deep and throaty. Diego played freely. His music sparkled across the night.

Below, the tourists began spilling onto the street, heading to their waiting buses. The mesmerizing music from the guitar drifted around them, and as if guided by a magic wand, they tourists came up to the terrace. Soon the *taberna* was humming.

Finally, after the last patron had left, the landlord opened two *Alhambras* and gestured over to Diego to join him at the bar. Diego pulled out a bar stool and sat down.

"How did that feel?"

"I don't remember much of it. But I know I liked it."

"That's how it was for me," the landlord said, chinking Diego's bottle. "¡Salud!"

"¡Salud!" replied Diego lifting the bottle to his mouth. "Why don't you play anymore?"

"Because I once believed I didn't deserve to, and now I've mostly forgotten how," replied the landlord. He took a sip of his beer and slowly straightened his stance. Thereupon he reached back for a bottle of whisky and poured himself a neat shot. "You'll join me in a nip," he continued gesturing with the whisky bottle.

Diego responded with a shake of his head.

"Sensible. It will rot your brain," said the landlord shuffling around to Diego's side of the bar counter and edging himself slowly onto a stool. He raised his glass at the doorway and in the direction of the Alhambra.

Through the gold filter of the whisky, the palace appeared as bright as the sun and the landlord remarked, "Even though its walls have been scaled and it's changed hands several times, do you think its purpose was ever questioned?"

"Umm, no, it's a magnificent fort."

"I've been looking across at it for as long as I can remember, and only recently did I figure out you don't leave a legacy by dwelling on your defeats and your mistakes. You learn from them, that's how you build stronger walls. What a fool I've been for taking so long to understand that."

"What do you mean? You have your own business."

"It's a bankrupted one. Tonight was the busiest it's been in years, thanks to you."

Diego didn't know whether to frown or smile. After a moment, he leaned back and, with a look of respect, he said to the man, "Tell me your story."

"You like sad stories?"

"It's your story and I'd like to hear it," said Diego firmly.

The landlord took a sip of his whisky then set his glass hard on the counter. "I once had a wife and a son who helped me run this *taberna*, but they gave up on me a long time ago. But they're not to blame, my moodiness and drinking drove them away."

Diego listened intently and the landlord continued. For many years, he'd sat all day on his terrace, only getting up from his spot when someone unexpectedly came into the tavern for a drink. He'd gazed down at the lives of others, riddled with regret and dwelling on the life that might have been.

As a young man, he'd been a talented guitarist and had begun making a name for himself by winning a few contests at the regional flamenco festivals. But when his big break came – an invitation to tour the country – he'd held back. The other guitarists he would have accompanied on the tour were a little older and more experienced, and he felt intimidated by them. Not only were they better guitarists, they also appeared to know the ways of the world. And he was just a teenager who'd never left Andalucía before. He'd kidded himself and his family he was going on the tour. Yet, even when he packed his suitcase, he knew he wouldn't be climbing aboard the train the next day. He pretended to himself the family *taberna* was his place in life.

His family waved him off on the morning of his impending departure and he headed in the direction of the train station. Though, at the first opportunity, he'd dived into a café and hid there until after the train was due to depart. He never did get back on the train of flamenco, deceiving himself for years that spending time with the flamenco people who frequented the *taberna* was as close as he needed to be to his dreams.

In time, he took over the bar from his ageing parents and, whilst the good times lasted, he made a success of it. But change crept in. Business people saw the growing opportunities to exploit Spanish culture for tourism. Many flamenco people moved away, and the caves became commercialised. The flamenco shows and the popular bars in the centre of the city became the big draw. Interest in his out of the way *taberna* dwindled and, as the business faltered, he began to drink more and neglect his family. Bitterness became his only company.

"I suspect that's how I'll be remembered," said the landlord, nodding at the bottle.

"Do you really care?"

"Not really," replied the landlord quietly. "No, that's a lie, I do care. But there's nothing I can do about it now. It's all too late."

Diego took a swig of beer and shared a half smile with the landlord. And the landlord continued talking.

"Son, don't have regrets. One path may not reveal roses but that doesn't matter. If it doesn't work out you can always turn around and try another path – you have to keep walking, that's the point."

Momentarily, Diego pondered on the man's words and then he said, "Can I buy you another drink?"

"*Gracias*, but no. It's been a long day."

THE LIGHTS WERE off, and Nadav had evidently gone to bed by the time Diego arrived back at the apartment. He entered his room, but he didn't need to turn on the light as a strip of pale moonlight painted the opposite wall. Diego sat down on the edge of the bed, staring at the silhouette of his half-emptied backpack and his guitar propped against the chair.

It would be nice to be in one place long enough to completely empty that bag, he mused. *But what if I keep walking? I've come this far.* He felt dizzy with his dilemma and he yanked off his boots. Then he tossed his hat onto the chair and fell back onto the bed.

He slept fitfully. A strong wind rattled the window and, in his dreams, he saw the silhouette of his father with his candyfloss cart, on the ridge of a hill under a turquoise full moon. Poplar trees bent in the wind, their tops brushing the moon. Then suddenly there was a boom of thunder, and thick clouds blacked everything out.

Diego leapt out of bed, the window was slamming back and forth in a violent wind and something was pelting the roof. He felt sand particles peppering his face as he forced the window shut and slumped onto the chair, putting his hands to his eyes.

Diego cleared the grains of sand from his eyes and began to relax as he listened to the wind rattling rhythms on the window and the roof. It brought to mind waves crashing onto a beach. He imagined them as thin ripples, gradually building across vast swathes of ocean, growing in stature as they absorbed the energy from the sun and the moon. *Is that not what was happening to me?* he surmised. Then suddenly, Diego realised that his heart had always been one step ahead: as soon as he'd set back out on the road, it had reconnected to the elements and believed in the possibility of his dream. And the people he'd encountered on the way had tapped into his heart. *They had felt it too,* he thought. And he now saw that people would always help you to get where you're going if they see that you were trying, if you demonstrated faith in a purpose. Just hours earlier, a depressed landlord had warned him about his own failings; even gypsies had done their best to assist him.

And Papá, yes Papá. What would he think of me now if I turned back? His backpack had been gathering dust for years, and now I've shaken it free. "¡*Madre mia!*" Diego exclaimed. "Keep walking *amigo*. Eventually, I'll find the right path."

He stood up, opened the window, stuck his head into the night and smiled as his hair flared behind his shoulders and the cool air filled his lungs. He remained there for a minute or two, seeing nothing, but realising everything, before he latched the window and went back to bed.

When Diego awoke a few hours later, sunlight the colour of yellow-ochre had replaced the moonlight on the wall. He got up and packed his bag. Then he took a quick shower, dressed and went into the kitchen.

He found Nadav sitting at the table, smoking a cigarette. In one corner of the room, there were a couple of sealed boxes, a lumpy duffle bag and the bouzouki.

"What's going on?" enquired Diego.

"I'm moving out."

"That was a hasty decision!?"

"Are you going to stand there gawping all day?" said Nadav pointing his cigarette hand at a coffee pot on the table. "You're making me feel uncomfortable."

Diego went over to a cupboard, grabbed a mug and then sat at the table.

"You've been busy. What time is it?" asked Diego, pouring himself a coffee.

"Lunchtime, I think."

"Gosh, I must have really slept."

"Didn't the storm keep you awake?"

"It woke me up for a little while."

"Hmm," said Nadav, taking a drag on his cigarette.

Diego drank some coffee, and looked expectantly at Nadav.

After a moment, Nadav said, "*Gracias*."

Diego raised his eyebrows and Nadav continued talking.

"For showing me the way."

"I did?"

Nadav explained that his night of merchandising had gone much better than he could have imagined. He'd avoided Plaza San Nicolás and gone straight to Paseo de los Tristes. He was nervous about playing the bouzouki, so instead he just set up his stall outside the gallery as usual. Trade was initially brisk, but then there had been a lull. And feeling bored, he began playing the instrument. Within a few minutes, he had drawn a small crowd who listened contently to his music, before buying his pictures. Subsequently, the owner of the gallery bought his remaining stock of photos. Nadav had returned to the apartment feeling exhausted, but elated. He couldn't sleep and, as he lay in bed listening to the storm, he had thought about everything that had happened since Diego's arrival just three weeks ago. Before then he'd become blind to so much.

"And I realised things are always much richer, if only we care to look. It's in the swaying of trees that we see the power of the wind. To understand the beauty of the rain, we have to look into the rivers and puddles to witness the patterns it makes, just as I experience those rare moments of life when I look through my camera lens. And I had never looked beyond me – I always saw myself as just a bitter soldier. But Diego, I am an artist. You believed it."

Diego winked casually at his friend. "So where's your profession taking you next?"

"I will return home to the Levant…"

"The Levant?"

"It's what they used to call the Eastern Mediterranean. There I will photograph its people, and show the world there is so much more beyond the appearances of war and conflict."

Diego gazed across the room, thinking about what Nadav had said. His words had reminded him why his journey was everything; there was so much more beyond its physical route. And then it struck him: *Inori* could be found in everyone and everything.

Nadav broke the silence and said, "Can I give you a lift to the station? I arranged for a mechanic to take my car to the garage this morning. It was just the alternator that had been the problem. And after all that time idle on the street, it just needed a new battery, an oil change and air in its tyres!"

"Unbelievable," exclaimed Diego. He took a sip of his coffee and said, "I've had a change of plan as well. I won't be going to the station."

"Didn't think you'd be hanging up your boots just yet."

"I'm going to continue my journey south, walking the Mozarábe Camino to guide me to Almería and the sea. It may not be Paco de Lucía's real homeland, but for some strange reason it still feels like the right path."

"I could give you a lift; it wouldn't take me too far out of my way."

"*Gracias*, but I want to complete the walk under my own steam."

"You're a stubborn one, Diego."

"Funny, that's what they used to say about my papá."

"Well, in that respect, you're clearly your father's son. Okay, at least let me take you to the outskirts of the city, and give you a head start along the trail."

"That would be perfect."

"And I need to give you your share from last night's takings; we did very well, selling all the stock to the lady at the gallery."

"That's not my money, last night you earned it yourself."

Nadav ignored Diego's remark, and pulled out a roll of bank bills from his shirt pocket. He counted through the bills, then pushed a handful forward. With a flick of his hand, Diego gestured to Nadav to put the money away, but Nadav continued to hold it out.

"A deal is a deal."

"Thought I was the stubborn one."

"Hmm," said Nadav shaking the money.

"Okay, okay," said Diego, taking it. "*Gracias*."

"Gather your things, the landlord already has plans to show someone the apartment later this afternoon, and I want to be gone before then."

Diego nodded, finished his coffee and washed his mug in the sink. Then he went into his room and opened his guitar case. He widened the instrument's strings across the sound hole and pulled out a thick roll of bills from inside the hollow of the guitar. He removed an elastic band from around them and added the latest money and counted through the whole wad. When he finished counting, he realised his small fortune was more or less equal to the amount of money he'd lost on the church steps in his village all those weeks before at the start of his journey.

Diego wrapped the elastic band around the bills and stuffed them back inside the guitar. Next, he collected his backpack and guitar case, then left the room.

"Leave your keys on the table and I've left you my contact details. Close the door hard behind you," said Nadav looking up as he collected the remaining box.

Diego placed his keys beside Nadav's set and picked up a scrap of paper on which Nadav had written his details. He folded the paper, put it in a back pocket of his jeans, and gave the kitchen a final glance. He went into the corridor and exited through the main door, pulling it firmly shut. Nadav was already at the end of the alley, turning a sharp corner, and Diego followed down behind him into a tarmacked street, where his Citroën was parked. Nadav put his boxes into the boot of the car while Diego put his packs across the back seat. Then they both got into the front of the car.

"Which way is the Camino path?" asked Nadav.

Diego shrugged his shoulders. "Um…"

"You'd never survive in the Israeli army!" remarked Nadav.

Diego smiled to himself. "Well, I came in from the north-west; maybe somewhere east of the city?"

"The trail would have to pass around the Sierra Nevada," replied Nadav. He squinted as he thought and turned the key in the ignition. "She sounds sweet, no?"

Diego smiled back at him, as the engine purred.

"Okay I have an idea," said Nadav as he let the handbrake down and the suspension of the car rose.

Nadav did a U-turn and drove up the hill, cursing as they edged their way past oncoming cars in the narrow streets. Before long, they had passed through Sacromonte, and were high above the city on a single-track road. Diego eyed the Alhambra below through the wing mirror. They approached a stone arch, with a decorative motif in the shape of a hexagram star on its keystone.

Nadav looked up at the star as they drove under the arch and said, "A sign to lead you on your way. Look around: do you see the footpath?"

Diego opened the window and scoured the immediate landscape but he couldn't see any Camino markers.

"I can't see anything. Maybe it would be easier if I go back to the centre. I've seen the signs in the alleys near the cathedral. I can work my way back from there."

"All that extra effort in this heat!"

"It could be a wild goose chase if I don't."

Just then, two male backpackers came around the bend ahead and ambled towards the car.

"Stop," said Diego, noticing a scallop shell swinging down from one of their backpacks.

Nadav pulled up beside the walkers and a fig tree.

Diego leaned out of the window. "*Hola*, are you walking the Mozarábe Camino?" he asked in Spanish.

The backpackers, two retired men, looked up at Diego curiously and Nadav interjected, asking in English, "You are on the path of the Camino?"

"Yes," replied one of the men a little out of breath. "We have just come down from the mountains. Are we nearly in Granada?"

"Not far, just keep walking all the way down the hill," replied Nadav.

Both men smiled gratefully.

"And the path is back that way?" continued Nadav, nodding up the road.

"Yes," said the other man, pointing back in the direction they'd just come with a walking pole. "The road narrows into a bridleway."

They thanked the pilgrims and the men resumed walking into Granada.

Diego was surprised at how much of the conversation he'd understood. Evidently, conversing with English speaking tourists in Madrid and Granada had improved his language skills more than he had thought.

"Well Diego, this is where our roads part."

"I guess so, *amigo*."

"I don't do sentimentality," responded Nadav.

Diego grinned. "That's okay, all photographers need to maintain a certain amount of decorum, especially IDF-trained ones."

Nadav stretched out his hand and Diego took hold of it. They shook with an unyielding respect for each other. Diego stepped out of the car and grabbed his belongings and afterwards peered through the passenger window at Nadav.

"Send me some photos."

"To where?" replied Nadav with a teasing smile.

"*Sí*, that's a very good question!"

"You have my number now."

"That's true. I'll message you when I next have a phone again – by then I should know."

Nadav started the car and winked at Diego before he turned around and drove back down the hill. Diego watched the car fade away. When it was out of sight, he pulled out his tobacco and rolled himself a cigarette. After smoking, he shouldered his backpack, adjusted the straps, gripped his case and began walking.

16

The Engineer

The afternoon sun was high, and in Diego's enthusiasm to continue his walk, he'd neglected to fill his flask or buy any food. Though, after a couple of kilometres, he heard the sound of trickling water through some bushes. A side path led him down to a stream with two white ducks swimming in it and a little further upstream there was a small waterfall. Its mist was a Mediterranean-blue.

Diego dropped his packs on the bank of the stream, and grabbed his flask. He pulled off his boots, rolled up his jeans and stepped into the cool water. The birds tilted their yellow beaks up at Diego before they swam over to the opposite bank and waddled out. Nonchalantly, they stretched their wings and flew away. Diego watched them disappearing into the sky before he walked upstream to the waterfall. Diego dipped his head into the tumbling water and shivered with pleasure as it washed over him. Wildflowers next to the waterfall nodded lightly. After a minute, he filled his flask. Then he went back to his things, put his boots on and continued on his way.

Not long after, he saw a man eating under the crown of a large chestnut tree, beside the ruins of a monastery. On seeing Diego approach, he stood up.

"*Buen camino*," yelled the lean man.

His hair was matted and silver wisps curled around the arms of his glasses.

Diego nodded and replied, "*Buen camino*." And on reaching the shade of the tree, he said, "*Con mucho gusto*."

"Greetings," replied the man. "My name is Jonathan."

"Diego."

"You're walking the Camino the wrong way?"

"Camino, *sí*."

"The correct way is towards Granada?" said Jonathan curiously.

"Granada," replied Diego, gesturing with his free arm in the direction he'd just come. "*Cerca*."

Jonathan looked blankly at Diego, not understanding Diego had said that the city was close.

"You British?" asked Diego, switching to his tourist English.

"English," said Jonathan with a nod. "And you're Spanish?" He gestured at Diego's guitar case. "Guitarist?"

"Yes. I am guitarist."

"Ah, I see you're a free spirit, a wandering guitarist!"

Diego nodded politely in response. Then Jonathan invited Diego to share his baguette and cheese lunch. Diego gratefully accepted, and they sat together under the tree and their conversation continued in broken English and the international language of gesticulation.

From what Diego understood, Jonathan had been a successful engineer, but he had recently sold his engineering company and retired. Diego noticed the signs of his wealth; his backpack was top quality and he was wearing a Rolex watch. Occasionally, he would check an app on his phone and, when Diego enquired what he was monitoring, Jonathan replied, "The markets."

Diego looked at him confused. Jonathan thought for a moment and said, "The Borse," gesturing with some fingers in the air and then he held his phone against his ear.

"Ah, *La Bolsa,*" said Diego. "You like numbers?"

"It's my gift, you might say. And yours is music no doubt," replied Jonathan nodding at Diego's guitar case and mimicking an air guitar.

"But why you walk *El Camino*?" asked Diego.

"My wife."

Then Diego discovered Jonathan was a workaholic. After selling his company, he sat all day in his study calling up his old work associates, meeting them for long lunches to talk about the good old days, and in-between, he'd play the stock markets. Finally, his wife had got angry with him, complaining their lives were no different in retirement than before. It reached a point where she asked him if he still wanted to be married. Jonathan had said he did, but his wife had retorted that he didn't know how to be a husband. Not long after that, Jonathan's wife had attended a talk about the history of the Camino de Santiago, which gave her an idea. She would persuade her husband to walk the Camino but gave him an ultimatum – if he still wanted to be married after walking it, he would have to sell all his stocks and forget about his former life as an engineer, and then they would share the rest of their lives together. If he couldn't do that, she would leave him.

"*¿Por qué?* I mean why you not enjoy life with your wife now?"

Jonathan shrugged his shoulders. "I need to protect the wealth I created."

"But what about your marriage?"

Jonathan fell silent, wondering why he'd said so much about his life to this stranger; it wasn't normally his way. But as he listened to the silence of the outdoors and the chirping of birds became more acute, he grasped that it was finally time to talk, and Diego was the first person he'd spoken to, beyond small talk, in at least a week; moreover opened up to in years.

He resumed talking and explained his wife was the love of his life, and that he'd met her at university but it'd taken him a long time to persuade her out on a date. But after that first date, they soon fell in love. However, they were from different backgrounds and her family didn't approve of their relationship. Nonetheless, they continued to see each other and, after they graduated, they secretly married. And it was then that Jonathan decided to prove to her family and the world that he was good enough. With his small savings and a bank loan, he bought a failing engineering firm and, within a couple of years, he'd turned it around and it was soon winning big international contracts from building highways to bridges and dams. In the process, they grew wealthy but Jonathan became wed to the business, rather than his wife. And though, in time, his wife's family acknowledged the wealth he had created, their acceptance continued to elude him. And so began a downward spiral; the more Jonathan sought their acceptance, the more he pushed the business and the less and less time he spent with his wife. And now that he'd finally retired, he and his wife were virtually strangers in their large house.

After they'd eaten, Diego made a cigarette and offered it to Jonathan, but he shook his head. Diego lit the cigarette and asked, "You still love each other?"

Jonathan smiled and said softly, "I believe we do."

"When was the last time you told your *señora* that?"

Jonathan's smile curled into a frown. "I don't remember."

Diego took a drag on his cigarette and then said, "You walk all the way to Santiago?"

"Yes, and after Santiago, I will continue the shorter Camino west to Finisterre. Coast to coast," replied Jonathan determinedly, before reaching for his phone.

"That is a very long journey across Spain! Who are you still trying to impress?" said Diego, interrupting Jonathan's focus on his share prices.

Jonathan put his phone down and looked up. "What do you mean?" he said opening his arms out.

"Jonathan, you having nothing to prove anymore. From where I sit, you are a very successful man, but I don't think you know how to really share. You share your food with me, but you don't share your life with your *señora*. Why are you not walking the Camino with her?"

"She wouldn't want to walk all that way?"

"You asked her?"

"No," answered Jonathan a little ashamedly.

Diego stubbed out his cigarette on his tobacco tin, and removed his hat. His belly was full and it felt good to stretch out across the grass. He looked up at the tree and its brown conkers splitting out of their spiky cases and swaying in the breeze. And through the quivering branches, he watched the only cloud in the sky being blown gently above the foothills of the Sierra Nevada. "We all need to help each other on our ways. Call your wife and ask her to join you."

"You speak very directly?"

"Life is short."

"Yes it is," whispered Jonathan.

"You can build bridges, but did you build a good marriage?" Jonathan fell silent and Diego continued talking. "As a team you achieve *muchísimo*, no? She can join you in either Granada or Cordóba?"

Jonathan bowed his head and thought for a moment. "You are right. I will call her," he said decidedly.

Diego sat back up and nodded gently at Jonathan in support.

"Can you make me a roll-up?"

"A smoke?" replied Diego.

"Please. I haven't had one in years but now I fancy one, just this once."

Diego made two cigarettes and they smoked in silence. After a while, the breeze picked up and they decided it was time to continue their respective journeys. They helped each other with their backpacks, shook hands and Jonathan said, "*Mucho gusto.*"

"*Mucho gusto,*" responded Diego.

He reached for his hat and mentioned where to find the waterfall. Jonathan reciprocated, explaining Diego's path would now take him up and across the foothills of the Sierra Nevada, for about 10km, before he'd reach a town and a hostel in its upper part. And with a smile and a friendly slap on Diego's back, he set off towards Granada.

Diego walked a few metres in the opposite direction and then glanced over his shoulder. Jonathan had stopped and was talking on his phone.

～

OLIVE TREES DOTTED a beige landscape of dry earth. The trail wound its way up towards two large, chiselled stone blocks in a wall that was missing its gate. A yellow Camino arrow was painted on one of the blocks and pointed back towards Granada. Diego paused to catch his breath and took in the scene. He was high up in a land of scrub and terraced hills. Southeast in the distance, waves of blue hills evaporated into a pastel blue and he guessed he was looking at the true Sierra Nevada mountain range. He drank some water and continued along the Camino; now a dusty track of red earth and crumbling stones. It made for steady walking and the smell of thyme, rosemary, sage and other heavily scented herbs wafted out from the scrubland, cleansing his nostrils and lungs as he breathed.

The sun was nudging the peaks of the Sierra Nevada by the time the trail turned and lurched downhill. Shadows from stone pillars and broken arches of a crumbling viaduct stretched up the path and towards Diego. It was still hot and Diego welcomed the shade. He was soon on the edge of Quéntar, and a bubbling stream beside a road led him uphill and into the heart of the town. Diego weaved his way up steep lanes and on each turn, he stopped briefly to catch his breath and look across the red-tiled rooftops of the staggered town. Smudges of cream and white buildings mingled with tall ferns and poplar trees, now splashed in the early colours of autumn. At the top of the hill, there was a sign with the word *Albergue*, and an arrow pointing up stone steps.

The hostel manager, a tall Swiss man, with the wrinkles of middle age, greeted Diego in the reception. The man handed Diego the guestbook and, as he filled out his details, he noticed a couple of lines above, next to yesterday's date, the name 'Jonathan Brown' and 'England'. Diego figured he would never meet Jonathan again, yet he would continue to cross the man's earlier footprints as he headed along the Mozarábe path to Almería. Meantime he hoped Jonathan would soon be making fresh footprints with his wife towards Santiago.

Diego treated himself to a private room, and as soon as he was shown to the single bed with its crisp cotton sheets, he pulled the curtains across the window, took a shower and then turned in. He was too tired to eat dinner.

When he awoke it was early morning and he heard chattering voices echoing from down the corridor. He got up, dressed quickly and headed for the kitchen. A group of pilgrims were eagerly eating, and Diego felt content making small talk with them. They told him it was a long walk to the next village, and so he didn't feel guilty about eating three pieces of banana cake with his hard-boiled eggs and toast. He drank a *café solo* with his breakfast. Before he left he bought a couple of *bocadillos* and more eggs.

Stepping out of the hostel, Diego squinted as the dawn sun slowly lifted over the tiled rooftops. He glanced at a plastic sign fixed to a telegraph pole pointing away from the hostel and back into town. It read: *Quéntar* and *Santiago de Compostela*. Diego turned against the sign and began climbing the hill. His legs felt stiff and he wondered if he'd ever get his walking fitness back. Suddenly from nowhere a dog bounded up to him with a stick in its mouth, which he rubbed against Diego's leg, urging him to throw it. Diego obliged and threw the stick up the hill and the dog chased after it and saw him to the edge of town.

He passed through groves of olive and almond trees and continued to climb towards a blue sky. It was relentless, and red earth track was already hot. Diego stopped often. Looking over his shoulder he was always impressed by how far away the valley and Granada had already become. He reached an abandoned chalk quarry, which stretched for a kilometre across the mountains and slowed his progress down as his ankles sank into soft dunes of chalk powder. The moonlike landscape finally led him to a cliff path, edged by squat pine trees with crowns like sombrero hats that provided some well-needed shade. Diego noticed an empty rifle cartridge on the path and the landscape changed again to a forest of tall pine trees. He felt he was passing through a land only pioneers and itinerants were *loco* enough to cross. His shoulders burned, his arm ached from carrying the guitar case, but nonetheless, he trudged on and up the zigzagging path.

By late morning the path hit a narrow forest road, which curved into a bridge across a wide gorge. Sitting on a stonewall by the roadside, he saw a man facing the pines, with a hunting rifle propped up beside him. As Diego approached, the man moved a finger away from the roll-up cigarette he was making and pressed it to his lips to indicate silence. Diego noticed an alertness in his dark eyes from under his baseball cap. He acknowledged him with a tip of his hat and went over and sat down beside him as the man finished making his cigarette.

"Lighter?" whispered the man.

Diego took out his lighter from a pocket, raising an eyebrow curiously at the man, but he didn't give anything away as he waited for Diego to light his cigarette. The grey flecks in his dark stubble sparkled in the sun. He reacted with a half-smile after Diego lit his cigarette. He took a puff and then passed it over to Diego. They didn't say a word as they shared the cigarette and, all the time, the brim of the man's cap pointed into the trees.

Just as they were finishing smoking they heard a twig snap. Diego saw the tips of two furry ears among the pines, and a deer poked its head out from between the trees. The man stubbed out his smoke on the wall and slowly stood up. He pulled his cap back so it sat high on his head, winked at Diego and collected his rifle. The deer's ears twitched and in a flash it was gone, its hooves bouncing off dry pine needles. Diego watched the man give chase and disappear up the slopes into the forest. He drank some water and continued on his way. Not long after he heard two rifle shots echoing across the gorge. He didn't look back.

The trees lining the road began to thin out and Diego tipped his Stetson low over his eyes against the midday sun. Soon there were no more trees, and all that remained were scorched stumps, charred earth, and one spared tree – a honey locust. Surveying the scene, he figured a forest fire must have spread through the area. Diego took his lunch under the shade of the lone tree's thorny branches.

The day continued in the mountains, and Diego walked on. When the sun began to drop, Diego looked about for somewhere flat to roll out his sleeping bag, but miraculously when he turned another bend a whitewashed village glowed into his vision. It was nestled in a narrow valley below. He spotted a limestone path that lead down to it. Cautiously he descended it into the village. A number of dogs lay patiently together in the last patches of sun outside a bar, waiting for their old owners playing cards and dominoes inside. Diego went into the bar and enquired about accommodation.

The landlady made a call, and shortly afterwards a fat woman of indistinguishable age, named Maricarmen, who was familiar to all in the bar, arrived with a set of keys in hand.

Maricarmen led Diego across the village to his accommodation, saying little, although when he remarked, "¡*Hace mucho calor!*" she replied it was always very hot in the summer, and that the village hadn't experienced any rain in two years. They arrived at the village school, and Maricarmen explained that during the summer holidays it doubled up as the local pilgrim hostel. She unlocked the main door and they went upstairs. There was a dormitory with half a dozen bunks and Maricarmen told Diego to choose a bed of his liking. She smiled and handed Diego the key. "Please return it to the bar when you leave in the morning."

That evening, Diego noticed the light still on in the village general store and bought some tobacco and food. He ate a dinner of bread, tinned tuna and half a packet of Chocowheel biscuits at a kindergarten desk. Afterwards, he picked up a piece of chalk and found himself writing in big letters across the blackboard, "Keep Walking Amigos".

Before he went to bed, he rinsed out the T-shirt and socks he'd been wearing that day and went outside into the playground. He hung his clothes out to dry on an improvised washing line erected for pilgrims. Then he placed a ten-euro bill in the pilgrim donation box, which was mounted on the wall inside the main door.

~

THE NEXT DAY, Diego cleared the mountains; although the land remained hilly, and the trail passed through gullies and was long and dusty. It proved to be another tough day of walking. And he was glad that he hadn't eaten all his bread and Chocowheels from the night before, as there weren't many places to buy food. The one restaurant in the only village he passed through was closed, and Diego lunched on the remains of his food and two Magnum ice creams bought at the post-office-cum-village-store, and snacked on the odd fig he picked on the way, each time delighting in their sun-ripened sweetness. As the day faded, and with no sign of a settlement on the horizon, he cautiously went into one of the abandoned cave dwellings, burrowed into the sides of the hill that had been dotting his pathway recently.

It was similar, but smaller, than the gypsy man-made cave in Pinos Puente he'd rested in. Niches had been carved into the whitewashed walls to form shelves and a cupboard. In one corner were rusting beer cans, plastic water bottles and a hand fan. Opposite lay a dusty single mattress. Feeling overcome with tiredness, Diego upended the mattress and beat off the dust. Then he laid out his sleeping bag across it, removed his denim shirt and boots, and crawled in.

～

DIEGO AWOKE AT dawn to the screeching of a bat and, in a bewildered panic of half sleep, he shooed it out of the cave. A light rain was tapping on the dry earth outside and the temperature had dropped. Diego fumbled around in the dimness for his shirt and put in on, and tightly wrapped his bag around himself and sat down. Momentarily, he struggled to find his breath, and his heart thumped like a galloping horse in his shivering body. It was like the time the thunderstorms came and his mother was no longer alive to comfort him. Diego felt very alone and, for the first time since throwing his phone from the bridge, he wished he had it. He would have spoken to anyone who would have answered his call. Diego didn't know how long he sat curled up and trembling, but eventually, he began to calm and he sensed a sugary aroma filtering through the musty cave. Sleepily he sniffed the air, then suddenly he sprang to his feet and out of the cave. Diego swung his head around in the thin dawn light and he glimpsed a man wheeling a candyfloss cart towards the riverbed below.

He eyed the man for a brief moment and then he was out of sight. Diego raced down the trail after him, in time to witness a mule pulling a cart across what was still, at this time of year, a dry riverbed. That section of the riverbed formed a junction of sorts – the opposite bank flattening out to a track leading away from the river. Diego rubbed his eyes and, when he removed his hands from his face, he noticed the cart was loaded with river cane. The cart and its load obscured the man leading it. Abruptly, the cart stopped and the man stepped to one side, dropping the reins of his mule. He was short and stocky and appeared elderly. The man massaged his hand, reached inside his jacket, and pulled out a hip flask. He unscrewed the cap and took a swig. All of a sudden the early morning mist spiralled up and around the cart, obscuring both man and beast.

"Papá?" yelled Diego incredulously into the haze. Then he felt the dampness of the morning's dew on the soles of his feet and realised he wasn't wearing his boots. He gazed again into the mist hanging over the dry riverbed and noticed a stream winding down its middle. Diego cursed to himself and dashed back to the cave, pulled on his boots and ran back to the riverbank, leaping clumsily over the stream and across to the other side. He ran up the track and tripped suddenly over his laces, which in his haste he'd neglected to tie. His splayed out hands broke most of the fall but as he got back onto his feet, his right ankle throbbed in pain. The final wisps of the dawn mist had now burned away. There was no longer any sign of the cart and Diego stood collecting his thoughts. It was *loco* to think he'd just seen Papá. *He's dead and buried.* Diego breathed in a large gulp of the morning air in an attempt to clear his muddled head, turned and hobbled back to the cave.

17

The Immigrant

Diego crossed the riverbed at the point where he'd witnessed the cart and, a couple of hours later, he limped into the small city. His ankle hurt, but nothing was going to stop him from reaching Almería and the Mediterranean. All that mattered was what was in front of him, and he didn't pay too much attention to the city's grand houses and churches. Although, if he had lifted his head high, he might have noticed the church with its plateresque portal, and an angel mounted between two ornamental pillars, resembling guitars in the morning shade. But he carried on along *Calle Santiago*, a cobbled street that led him out of the centre.

Diego wanted to get out of the highlands as soon as possible, though he stopped briefly for breakfast and to stock up on food at a café. Mounted high in the corner was a boar's head, and on the wall behind the counter a photo of the proprietor, dressed in hunting slacks, standing proudly with his rifle. When Diego paid his bill, he enquired about a pharmacy. The proprietor said there was one further up the street and suggested he might try, arnica. Diego went to the pharmacy and purchased the arnica gel. Outside, he rubbed the gel on his swollen ankle and miraculously, after a short distance of walking, the swelling had receded. Diego smiled with relief and strode on.

THE NEXT COUPLE of days were long and arduous and, although there were clouds in the sky, strong rays of sunlight seeped through every gap. Diego tipped his Stetson low over his forehead and filled his flask with water at every opportunity. Accommodation was a hit and miss thing. He'd slept in the backroom of a *taberna* in a former mining town one night and the next night he spent it in a twee bedroom, courtesy of the town mayor. However, Diego was awoken on the hour, every hour, by the clocktower bells in the adjacent church.

IT HAD BEEN six days in the hilltops after leaving Granada and Diego was relieved to find the trail winding down from the high plateaus and into the valley of wind turbines. He'd been eyeing their immense presence on the landscape in recent days, and now their continuous whirring carried Diego along the lush valley. Eventually, he noticed a painted Camino arrow pointing away from the dried up riverbed. Diego crunched along the riverbed for a few kilometres before noticing another arrow sprayed on a boulder pointing down from an opening in the riverbank, beyond which he spotted a church steeple poking above a hedgerow of fig trees. Suddenly, the sound of jangling bells bounced around the riverbanks and a herd of goats filtered past him. An elderly man wearing a baseball cap popped up from in amongst them and shouted, "*Peregrino?*" above the din of bells and bleating animals.

Diego smiled. "*Sí Señor.*"

The goat herder lifted his staff and pointed up to the clouds now hanging low over the river. "*Amigo*, be careful. Much rain is expected and these dry rivers can fill rapidly in a sudden rush. Where the banks are high, there is no escape. It doesn't rain for most of the year, but when it comes it's treacherous." He nodded at a goat. "Every time I lose a goat that wanders too close to the river."

"*Gracias* for the information," replied Diego.

The goat herder reached into the pocket of his woollen shirt and pulled out a notebook and pencil. "I will draw you a map of an alternative route." He stepped around his goats and over to Diego. The man was short, but his limbs were solid, like he'd been chiselled from the rocks that lined the riverbank.

"Which way are you heading?" asked the man.

"To Almería."

"Ah, you walk the royal road, *Camino Real*."

Diego viewed the goat herder with curiosity.

"Queen Isabella and King Ferdinand came this way when they took back Spain from the Moors. That was beginning of the end for Spain."

"It was?"

"The Moors brought us culture, and then we destroyed it all like we destroy everything, for gold and silver," he continued as he went about drawing the map in a page of his book.

Within a couple of minutes, the goat herder had drawn a map, torn out the page and handed it to Diego. The map was a piece of art. The river was drawn with fine curves and scattered along it were old farmhouses and settlements. A steep path swirled up from the river to a road above. At the top of the road were rows of

trees, drawn the shapes of lollipops, and a stick figure
of a man with a guitar, and an arrow pointing along
the winding road towards a village plaza and church
indicated by a shaded square and a cross. The village's
name was 'Alboloduy.' Above the road were flowing
lines, indicating the steep gradients of higher hills.
Past Alboloduy, a stone marker had 'C' scribbled on it,
indicating Camino, with an arrow pointing back to a big
bend in the river. And to the side of the map, in block
capitals, the goat herder had written: +6.5 KM.

"You understand?"

"*Sí*, an extra 6.5km via the road and a steep climb,"
answered Diego.

"*Exactamente, amigo.*"

The goat herder put two fingers to his mouth and
whistled a sharp shrill at his dogs and one rounded the
goats up, while the other, a brown and white German
Shepherd, paused in the middle of the riverbed and
glared intensely at Diego, showing him his fangs before
clipping at the heels of a straying goat. Diego observed
the last of the goats rounding a bend in the river and
stood in the middle of the riverbed until he could no
longer hear their bells. He folded the paper and put it
in a pocket beside his passport. Then he looked up at
the steeple above the hedgerows, hoping he might find a
restaurant in the village that could cook him up a steak.

It was more of a small town than a village. Diego
passed a couple of bars, and peeked into both. Neither
tempted him. They were dingy and occupied by young
men either sitting at the bar counter or gathered around
the fruit machine. The bars reminded him of Madrid's
seedier drinking holes, and he sensed they wouldn't
provide a decent meal. He continued up into the town

past a chapel and emerged into a quiet plaza with old men sitting and chatting across from each other on two benches. There was a friendly-looking *taberna* with vines and purple bougainvillaea crawling up its stonewalls. On closer inspection, Diego was disappointed to discover a sign on the door stating that it was closed for two weeks. Diego turned to the local store and decided the steak would just have to wait. He hadn't seen anywhere else to eat in the town's upper parts, and he didn't like the look of the lower town.

Diego bought Manchego cheese, a baguette and a bag of crisps. As an afterthought, he added a can of cold beer and more tobacco to his supplies. Next, he thought about finding somewhere to sleep. He looked about and spotted on the corner of a building a sign for an *Albergue*, indicating towards the top of the town. Diego climbed the hill and was soon standing on the steps leading up to the hostel's door. Though its door was locked, there was a notice with a telephone number to call for the key. Diego shrugged his shoulders but he wasn't that concerned: he had no phone and couldn't call the number. He turned around and appreciated the spectacular view across from the hills to the dry river below. Then he dropped his pack and guitar on the tiles of the porch, sat on a step and began making himself a cheese and crisps *bocodillo*. After he'd eaten, he washed it down with the beer and rolled himself a cigarette. The sun dipped behind the hostel and the clouds whipped around the hills and glowed a dull rose. In one cloud, he saw the shape of a ram's head. Then the winds came. Diego rolled his sleeping bag across the tiles of the porch, removed his boots and climbed in.

～

WHEN HE AWOKE early the next morning, the sky was a swamp of dark clouds and the wind whistled around the hostel door. Diego sat up and pulled his bag tight around him. It wasn't raining yet, though he smelled the damp in the air and his instinct was to inquire about access to the hostel and stay until the rain had passed. But he also figured that if the rains were as bad as the goat herder had suggested, he would be stuck there for days and the last thing he wanted to do was to give his drinking vice any excuse. Too long there and he might be sucked into those miserable-looking bars.

Diego jumped out of his sleeping bag, and went around the back of the hostel and took a pee. Next, he washed his hands and face with the water from his flask, and took a deep glug from what was left. He sat back down, batted away an annoying fly, pulled on his boots and gathered his things.

Diego marched down the hill with an eye on the threatening clouds. Judging if he kept up this pace, he would beat the rain, avoid circumnavigating the river and he'd soon arrive in Alboloduy. But as soon as his feet crunched onto the riverbed, he felt a couple of drops of rain bounce off his Stetson. He looked up at the road just as a fork of lightning lit up the top of the hills, trailed by the trembling roar of thunder. Diego shuddered and fumbled in his pocket for the map the farmer had given him and studied it for a while. Another flash crackled across the treetops and he stuffed the map into a back pocket of his jeans. He quickly shouldered his pack and, gripping his guitar case, darted downstream along the riverbed.

The rain came in swathes, pushing Diego to one side of the riverbank for protection. He rushed along in a panic and didn't notice a stone marker at the point at which the riverbed split and he chased down the narrower channel. Diego arrived at an area where bamboo vegetation had sprung up thickly and blocked the way forward. A stream began bending around his boots and the wind cut through his shirt. Water poured off his hat and he pushed the bamboo away and waded under its canopy hoping to find a sign to redirect him.

The water swelled around his ankles and he became more lost in the undergrowth of the bamboo. Eventually, he beat his way through to a ravine where the shale had eroded to sand and the banks were solid overlapping boulders, forming a catchment basin of sorts. Stencilled on one boulder was the ubiquitous Camino arrow with the scallop shell symbol seemingly pointing back into the undergrowth. Abruptly, the cicadas and birds fell silent. Diego sensed the unstoppable power of the water, and he turned his head back in the direction of the arrow. The bamboo bent like grass in the wind and a foaming torrent of water at waist-height rushed downstream towards him. He sprang onto the edge of one boulder and stretched his free arm forwards to grab a bamboo stem on the side of the bank. But he slipped on the wet rock and dropped his guitar case and it bounced off the boulder and into the river. "*Cabrón*," yelled Diego. As he adjusted his position to see where his precious guitar was going, his ankle twisted awkwardly and he skidded off the rock falling backwards into the deluge.

He felt his bottom bounce off the riverbed, and his head popped up above the water like a buoy. His hat was carried away in the flow towards a narrow gorge-like gap. Momentarily, he relaxed and observed what was happening. The Camino arrow had disappeared under the rising water line and he was trapped in the basin. Diego figured he had to find a way to scramble up the rocks at the side. He tried swimming towards them but the strong flow pulled him towards the gap and his backpack obstructed his arms. He felt his energy leaving him, and he slipped his arms from under the straps of his pack and it was instantly dragged away by the current. Diego tried again and again for the rocks on his left side, but each time he reached them, his hands slid off their glasslike surface, and he was pulled back into the flow. Summoning all his strength he swung his arms violently and kicked as hard as he could towards the right bank, where there was more foliage to grip, but as he did a log slammed into his side, thumping the wind out of him. Diego floated on his back, slowly rotating, and gasping for air. Looking up at the heavens, he said to himself, *Let God decide.*

The force of the water carried him towards the gap. His body was pushed and twisted through it and then pulled under its cascade, and dragged downstream and into the main river, where it was wider but now no deeper than waist height. Diego's knees scraped across the pebbled bottom and he found he was able to stand. The water knocked him over a few times, but each time he pulled himself back up to standing. He staggered across to a bend in the river where he could see it levelled out into a dry bank of sand and scree. Then he fell onto the sand and after a minute rolled himself into a ball and, with his arms wrapped tightly around his knees, sat hypnotised watching the water. It was a force of nature to be treated with respect but, at that moment, Diego despised its unpredictable menace.

He was freezing and shivering uncontrollably in the relentless rain. For a moment he scrunched his eyes shut, and all he thought of was Papá. If he'd been around, he'd never have allowed Diego to have been caught out like that.

"*Hola*," whispered a voice from above.

Diego opened his eyes in surprise and looked up. Through the rain, he glimpsed an African man leaning over him. The African held out his dripping guitar case. Diego nodded meekly. The man reached out a hand and Diego grasped it and he was pulled to his feet. He noticed the African had nothing but the sodden clothes he was wearing and a bedroll he carried under his arm. His hair was thick and wiry and he was wearing a Spiderman T-shirt, a pair of shorts and rope-soled shoes. Diego's eyes adjusted further and he realised the African was no older than a teenager.

"Where did you just come from!?" asked Diego.

The teenager smiled to avoid appearing rude for not fully understanding him and handed Diego his guitar case. Then he gestured to a hedgerow of bamboo and he led Diego through it to a clearing, and the Camino path that wound its way uphill. Diego limped wearily behind the teenager. They passed a stone shack attached to which, hung a trellis of grape vines straddling the path. Beside the shack was a bench and they sat down to shelter from the direct force of the rain. Diego continued to shiver and, after a couple of minutes, he stood up and peered through the mesh window of the shack. It was dim but he could see no one was inside, and what's more there was a pile of firewood next to the wood burner. He went to try the door handle and the African shook his head. The door was locked.

Diego sat back down, wiped the damp off his guitar case and tentatively opened it up. Water was splashed across the guitar's body but, on closer inspection, it appeared unharmed and generally dry. He pulled out the roll of bills from within the sound hole and they were also dry. Subsequently, he checked his passport in his pocket. It was sodden but still legible.

Diego put the money and his guitar away. He would have spent all that money on a hotel room and hot shower at that moment. Then he noticed the teenager was also shaking. Diego stood up and went to the door again and the teenager's bright eyes curiously followed him. Diego turned his body and slammed into the door with all of his weight, screaming with pain from the bruises the log had given him.

The door shook on its hinges but remained firmly shut. The teenager stood up and stepped beside Diego and turned his shoulder to the door. "*Uno, dos, tres,*" said Diego and, together on the three, they slammed into the door and, with a crunch, it flew open and they were in. Diego grimaced with pain, but he was glad to be inside. They found matches beside the wood burner and soon it was crackling with large flames and both of them had removed their shirts and were sitting close to the fire on two folding fishing chairs they'd found in the shack. Their shirts, Diego's socks, his passport and the teenager's blanket hung above the burner from a clothesline.

There was no food in the shack, but they munched on large tomatoes the teenager had been carrying and grapes from the trellis. The shack soon became cosy and it didn't take them long to dry out. With his energy restored, Diego looked over at the teenager and said, "*Gracias.*"

The young African looked curiously back at Diego, not sure why he was being thanked. Diego responded with a smile and gestured to his guitar, which he'd removed from its case and had propped up in a corner to dry out any lingering moisture. The teenager acknowledged Diego with another smile.

"How did you know?" said Diego, trying to communicate in his tourist English.

The teenager replied, "Know?"

"*Si,*" said Diego, gesturing playing the guitar with both his hands and then nodding back at his guitar.

"Ah, I cross bridge and see guitar in river," said the teenager in broken Spanish. "I think who it belong and I go down river and see you."

"Lucky me," replied Diego smiling. "You not see a *mochila*?"

"*Mochila*?"

Diego curled his fingers and put his hands to his shoulders, gesturing the shouldering of a backpack. The teenager understood, but shook his head.

"That's okay, I have my guitar," said Diego, though he regretted losing the photos of his mother and father. "Where are you going?"

The teenager understood and replied in a language Diego didn't understand, although its tone sounded strangely familiar. Noticing Diego didn't comprehend, the teenager looked about the sparse shack. He spotted some old fishing rods, tackle and a fraying net in a corner. He got up from his chair and picked up one of the rods and feigned casting it while he made a rolling motion, like ocean waves, with his other arm. Diego realised he was mimicking fishing from a boat. The teenager said, "*España, trabajo.*"

Diego understood he was an immigrant, who had come to Spain for work, most likely smuggled illegally by a fishing vessel. "You work in Spain?" said Diego.

"*Sí*, close to Almería. Agriculture. Very hot, very hard. I not be slave there."

"But where do you go for work now?"

"Madrid," said the teenager.

"Very far," said Diego, making a broad sweep with an arm.

"Not far, I walk Camino there."

"You know *El Camino*?"

The teenager nodded and Diego smiled back at him, and then glanced up at his blanket and T-shirt drying above the burner. *That's all he has*, he thought. And then he remembered how strangers had helped him on his own road. Diego stood up and retrieved his guitar from the corner and poked his hand inside its sound hole and pulled out the roll of bills. It was fourteen hundred and some odd Euros. He put the odd Euros into his pocket and discovered the arnica gel also in his pocket. Then he held out the fourteen hundred Euros to the teenager. The teenager stiffened and pushed the money back with his long fingers.

Diego felt embarrassed and he stuffed the money back into the guitar. "*Suerte.* Good luck," was all he could think to say. Then he walked over to the door and looked out. It was still damp but it had stopped raining. He took out the arnica and rolled up his right trouser leg and applied some gel to his ankle, then to the bruising on his chest. After he reached for his shirt from the line and, finding it was dry, he put it on. The teenager dressed, collected some items from a corner and rolled them up into his blanket. Afterwards, he beat out the fire with a stick he found amongst the logs.

Diego finished dressing, left some bills in the shack in gratitude and together they found a large stone and put it against the bottom of the door to prevent it from swinging open. They shook hands then Diego turned left up the path and the teenager right.

The air was cool and Diego hugged himself with his free hand, thinking the first thing he would do in the next town, would be to buy a new sleeping bag, or failing that a thick blanket. He stopped momentarily, opened his case and pulled out the roll of bills from the guitar. Diego turned around and ran after the teenager. "*¡Espera!* Wait," he shouted out after him. The teenager stopped and turned around. Puffing Diego showed the youth his money and pointed to the blanket he held rolled under his arm. Diego beat his spare arm around his chest and shivered. "*¡Frio!* Very cold!" Diego held out the money again. The teenager reached out a hand and took the money and passed over the bedroll to Diego with a slight nod, but he couldn't meet him in the eye.

"*Gracias*," said Diego.

"*Jazāk Allāhu Khayran*. May the Almighty reward you," replied the teenager before he turned and continued walking.

The path etched into the side of the hill and led Diego up to moorland and then across to a section of the road that he would have met earlier if he had followed the goat herder's map. The clouds began to disperse and the arnica had again eased his discomfort. Thankfully, the walking was easy compared to what Diego had been used to. The road soon descended towards a bridge that crossed the river to a town that he figured must be Alboloduy. He crossed the bridge, but didn't care to look down at the river below.

Bunting hung above the streets of whitewashed buildings, the sign of a recent festival. It was tempting to stop there for a while, but his walking was good and Diego wanted to take advantage of the tarmacked single-road that followed the river. A finely chiselled stone Camino marker pointed back into the town. He walked against it, and soon the road gave way to a path that ascended gentle hills, bronze and scraggy with the odd cactus. The rains had brought out the wildflowers, sprinkling the landscape in vibrant blooms of red, white and yellow.

Diego figured he wasn't far from the coast now, and he kept up his pace into the late afternoon, only stopping briefly at a bar. He spent the last of his money on tapas, a bottle of water and a lighter. Then when the sun began to fade, he found himself at another river, where a Camino arrow pointing upstream had been crudely painted onto a boulder. The riverbed was very wide, with low banks and only a tiny stream flowed down its middle. Diego stopped to pick up a stone from the dry riverbed. It felt rough and bone-dry. He dropped the stone and crunched downstream with renewed vigour. The shadows from industrial greenhouses lining the riverside leaned into the riverbed and grasshoppers jumped about in the thick grass at its edges. Not long after, Diego spotted wide tyre marks from a vehicle heading out of the river and onto a track; he left the river and his path led him under a railway line. When he emerged from the underpass, he found himself in a municipality above Almería just as the sun finally went down. Lights twinkled across the undulating city below. Diego felt a chill in the air and figured Almería and his quest could wait until tomorrow. He walked about the suburban neighbourhood and came across a grassy football pitch. This was as good a place as any to lay out his African friend's blanket.

He shook out the blanket and from it, something dropped onto the grass. Diego knelt down and picked it up. It was a rolled up prayer rug and inside it, he found a photograph, a hair comb and a single drumstick. *That was stupid of me*, Diego thought. *Not to have checked the blanket to see if anything was rolled inside it*. But the exchange had felt awkward and Diego had continued briskly on his way to save the teenager any embarrassment. He picked up the picture and looked at it in the last light. It was a black man, unsmiling but proud, wearing a rimless cloth hat and holding an infant. Diego began to cry. He had never cried for someone else before.

After he had wiped away the last of his tears, Diego draped the blanket around his shoulders like a poncho and made himself a cigarette. He felt grateful that the tin had protected his tobacco from the water and for having the blanket. Diego smoked, meditatively looking up at the millions of bright stars above, thinking he had come a long way because the Milky Way was no longer overhead and guiding him as it had done to Santiago. Soon after, he stretched across the grass, wrapped himself in the blanket and fell into a deep asleep.

18

In the Desert

Diego awoke to a cool Mediterranean breeze. And in
that first dawn of the day, he felt in his bones that,
for whatever reason, everything would be different after
reaching the sea. His walk would be over.

He cupped some water from the bottle he'd bought
and splashed it onto his face. Then he took a long,
measured drink. After he rolled up the blanket with the
African's items inside it, he collected his guitar case.
As he walked with his case dangling from one arm and
the bedroll under his other arm, he wondered if anyone
would look at him and think he was a hobo. But Diego
didn't care, he was a pilgrim, and he felt as rich as any
man could be. And as he walked he pulled some figs
from a fig tree and ate them gratefully.

Diego was soon on the edges of the city and he
began seeing many yellow arrows pointing away from
the centre and in the direction he'd just come. Cutting
through a plaza, he eyed a bronze statue of a male
guitarist sitting on a wall. *I knew it*, Diego speculated. But
on closer inspection, the guitarist was wearing spectacles
and was evidently John Lennon. Diego could not help
himself from laughing loudly, arousing the attention
of passers-by and the waiters who were setting up for
the day at their terraces. He had no idea why Lennon
was associated with the city, but that didn't matter. His
statue was the next best thing to Paco de Lucía. If he'd

had his phone, he would have taken a photo of Lennon and sent it to Nadav.

When he finally composed himself, he continued through the city and along an elegant avenue lined with trees clipped into the shape of Cossack hats, before they gave way to palm trees, a marina and the sea. Diego skirted around the marina to the beach. Fish restaurants lined the walkway, and already sun umbrellas were popping up across the sand. As his father could never afford holidays or didn't care for the beach, Diego had rarely been to the seaside. He sat down on the low wall edging the sand, whipped off his boots and socks, rolled up his jeans and strode excitedly across the sand to the water's edge. Dropping his things he stepped into the sea. The water lapped around his ankles and he could feel the salty water healing his damaged ankle. Diego stood for a long time observing the sea's sparkling, rippling surface all the way out to a misty blue horizon. Had he expected to see Africa? A miracle? He didn't know. All he knew was standing there in the sea felt good and, after a while, he stepped a little further in until he was knee deep, and remained standing there without a thought for a few minutes until he felt the current pulling at his feet. He looked right at the high-rises, then left at the bay curling into a turquoise ocean. Diego stepped out of the water, collected his possessions and headed along the beach towards the serene colour.

He wasn't sure why he had resumed walking; it wasn't out of habit, and certainly, Diego knew he could do with a good rest. But he'd felt a little uncomfortable in the urban world again, and the more he walked along the bay the calmer he felt. There was no way around the end of the bay, without swimming around the rocks, so Diego cut across the sand to the road hugging the coastline. He put on his boots and walked along the road, passing the city airport, palatial-looking hotels, and dense greenhouses, like a tented city, along which a roadside community lived where Arab-looking men cycled past him turning their heads curiously as they went by. After a while, the road turned inland and the landscape changed. It was an arid orange-ochre world, where extinct volcanoes hung in the distance, and aloes with spiky leaves and tall flowers lined the road like green telegraph poles. He marched on, and the road cut back down to the sea and to a small seaside resort, but it didn't delay him. Diego found a path leading up jagged cliffs and he continued southeastwardly, watching the sun carpet the sea as he walked.

He turned his shirt collar up against the burning sun and, with unrelenting strides, strode on through a barren landscape, possessed by something, but he did not know what. On one outcrop, a lighthouse stood like the last settlement in the world, and Diego noticed someone had sprayed a red cross on its tower, similar to the cross of the Knights of Santiago, and that only served to push him onwards. An avenue of aloes led Diego down a steep ridge to pristine, untrodden beaches. He removed his boots again and walked along the shoreline.

By lunchtime, he'd drunk the last of his water, but as he looked back at his footprints in the sand, he felt his journey was not over yet. Dusk found Diego on another cliff edge beside an 18th-century fort, looking back out to sea and watching the sun slowly sinking beneath puffy clouds, hanging low on the horizon and caught in the sunset show. Further up the coastline, he spotted a thin peninsula and a modest bay, blanketed in golden shadows from the sun's final rays. Diego decided he would stop there that night and see what came of it.

The fishing village had several beaches either side of the peninsula to choose from, but Diego chose the first one where several small fishing boats had been dragged up the beach. A breeze was coming off the sea and Diego rolled out his blanket on the leeward side of an aging skiff and sat leaning against it. The sea air washed over him and, in the silence, he had the feeling he wanted to play his guitar. He removed it from its case, hoping that it sounded as good as before its dunking in the river.

Diego buried his feet in the sand and rested the guitar on his leg. For a moment, he just sat there, watching the waves now tinged amber by the sunset and listening to the pebbles on the shoreline rubbing together, clicking like castanets. He closed his eyes, drew the guitar into his chest and breathed in deeply as the Mediterranean Sea heaved into the land; exhaling as he felt it pulling deep towards Africa and flowing onto the Levant. And in that moment, he felt no space between those distant continents and himself.

He felt the tensions of the strings, and turning his left hand crabwise, his fingers crawled along the frets of the instrument. Surf fizzed across the beach, and he found he was able to tap out its spray onto the soundboard of his guitar. The gusts of wind and the suck of the sand he shaped into flat and forlorn chords. He opened his eyes, lifted his head and turned to face the sea. The final light of the sun glowed across the water and onto the blurred smudges of rocks at the sea's edge. His playing hand brushed across the strings. Diego didn't feel the urge to sing. What came was just an even-tempered hum, vibrating from deep inside him. He was a bird climbing the thermals, desolate and wordless; reflective but poised. It was the truest song he had ever played.

When the tide had turned and withdrawn again, in its silence, he remembered what Daniel had said back in Madrid: "The best carpenters sharpen their tools in the woods." Only now did he understand what his friend had meant. *Just as holy men of every faith retreat to the wilderness, it is only in solitude that one can become pure enough to be the vessel of God's voice.* The drink, the lust, the self-pity, even the chasing of fame was a false note. Diego had never been in tune with just who he was. "Am I finally clean?" he whispered.

But, in his heart of hearts, he knew he wasn't; even at that moment, he would have loved a beer with the cigarette he was about to roll. Diego finally understood that without his guitar he would be always out of tune – he must always keep his passion for playing it. It was his lifeline, the instrument to help him with his own form of praying, his *inori* that would keep his faith alive.

Diego felt exhausted, and rested a cheek on the hip of his guitar as the sea drew him further into its spell. Sometime later, he sat up and made himself a cigarette. As he sat smoking and looking at the half moon poised above the sea, he decided to bury the items he'd found rolled into the blanket. He dug a deep hole in the sand and rolled them into the prayer matt. As he patted the sand over them, he thought of the teenager one day returning to Africa as a successful businessman, and being reunited with his father and family. After that, Diego began writing a note in the sand to his own departed father; thoughts about his journey but also words that had gone unsaid. He ended the note with the following words: *And one day, when I join you in that house in the sky, I'll tell you this story of my Camino.*

Diego hoped his father might look down from the heavens and see what he'd written before the sea washed it away. But even if Papá never read his note, he felt better for writing it. Diego stood up and got into the boat, wrapped the blanket tightly around himself and was soon asleep.

~

GRUFF VOICES AND the sound of wood on sand aroused Diego. He sat up suddenly and witnessed fishing vessels landing on the beach, surrounded by seagulls. The sky was full of rose-tinted clouds. As he gazed up the beach he saw the silhouettes of hardy men attaching cables to their small boats and winching them up the sand. They didn't pay too much attention to Diego, and he turned his head back to the shoreline. As his eyes adjusted to the thin light, he had the feeling the panorama looked familiar, but was unsure why. Observing the rocks more closely, he noticed one was slightly remote from the others. It had been chiselled by the sea and wind into the shape of a resting camel looking out to sea. Then he knew where he'd seen a similar view before. It was the mural on the shutters of the fishmongers, across from the flamenco school in Madrid. The school he hadn't had the courage to enter.

He saw the silver glint first before a marlin broke the surface of the water. It hung like a crescent moon in the air for a moment, before disappearing soundlessly into the waves. Diego looked at the fishermen but they hadn't seen the fish and were continuing to drag their boats to shore and unload their catch. That was the final sign; *a gift*, he thought. Diego now knew what he must do. He would return to Madrid and walk boldly into that flamenco school and perform his audition like his life depended on it. He would first learn the rules, and then break them like a true artist.

Diego supposed the fishermen would soon be taking coffee or something stronger at a local restaurant and seeing they had a fine catch, he hoped they would tip generously after the guitar performance he was about to give them. He needed enough money to get back to Madrid. Diego climbed out of the skiff, collected his guitar and walked up the beach towards the village beyond.

Epilogue

Diego took the same table as before at the café across the street from the indoor market with the flamenco school above it. The waiter took his order of a mineral water and a sandwich. He wasn't deliberately delaying crossing the street this time; he hadn't eaten since his early performance at the fish restaurant, and then he had slept most of the train journey to Madrid.

He ate his lunch and told himself he could have a cigarette after the audition. There was a familiar grating sound from behind him. He put his glass of water down, and looked over his shoulder expectantly. Again, there was the fishmonger lowering the shop's shutter and locking up for *siesta*. Diego smiled knowingly, as he observed the same panorama he'd witnessed just earlier that morning, only now it was in the form of a mural. He stood up, picked up his guitar case and paid his bill. He glanced across to the spiral staircase leading up to the school, visible through the building's glass entrance, before he took a step towards the street.

Diego passed through the doors of the building, and as he prepared to head up the staircase, he turned his head towards the market. It was bustling with people, like a city back in business after a long, hot summer. He returned his attention to the flamenco school above and began climbing.

As he neared the top of the stairs, he recalled the advice Papá had always given him when deciding what style to perform. He stopped. *How do I feel?* He took a deep breath and momentarily closed his eyes. What came to mind was the marlin glistening in the cool dawn air. Diego felt completely free. He gripped his guitar case tightly and grinned to himself. He was ready.

Have you read the first story in the Reluctant Pilgrim series?

Candyfloss Guitar

is out now at:

Amazon.com
Amazon.co.uk
Amazon.in

And all of Amazon's international sites

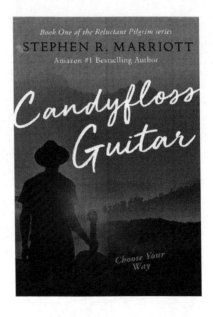

Extract from Candyfloss Guitar – The Reluctant Pilgrim #1

Eduardo's mind then turned to Diego and his friends drinking the night away, reassuring themselves in between their glugs of beer, "there are no jobs out there". His shoulders and neck muscles ached as he asked himself what had happened to that enthusiastic boy, eager to try everything and always wanting to learn a new chord or a different way to pluck the strings. But again, he couldn't answer the question and he became aware of all the sounds in the house in anticipation of the creaking door and stairs that marked Diego's return in the early hours. So Eduardo did not go back to bed; instead he went to his wardrobe and, pushing to one side a row of fading flowery dresses, he reached for the long dark neck and fine smooth curves of what had once been his substitute for love.

Eduardo sat back down on the stool, crossed his legs and gently rested the pale cypress guitar on his top leg. He ran the fingers of his left hand up the ebony fingerboard and with his free thumb he stroked the strings in a slow downward motion. He then rested his index and middle fingers on adjacent strings but as he tried to pluck them his hand cramped up and froze. Eduardo didn't try to continue. Ignoring the creaks in his back, he rose to his feet. And an ailing tone resonated around the room from the fallen guitar as Eduardo opened his lungs and cried into the night, "Qué Cabrón! Why?"

As the moon disappeared behind clouds, Eduardo made his decision. He left the room and headed downstairs to the phone.

It was only when Eduardo felt the warm paving slabs outside the Post Office that he realised he wasn't wearing his shoes. But the storm inside him swelled and he stumbled on in the night and in the direction of Bar Paradiso. On the fringes of the plaza, Eduardo fell to his knees and gasped for air. For a few moments there was nothing but darkness and silence, suddenly broken by a pulsating rhythm. Eduardo felt himself coughing and his body being pulled up by the sound. The racing beats turned to a slower, more sensual melancholia that Eduardo recognised from his past, which drew him closer to its source.

The outside of the bar was dim and the dancing gathering partially masked Eduardo's view. But he still recognized the tall outline of the man holding the guitar like a man embracing his tango partner. The familiar bittersweet music was being played by his son. It was Diego.

The crowd cried out for more but Diego shrugged his shoulders and handed the guitar back to Arnau. Eduardo took a couple of steps closer but stopped before the light of the bar revealed his presence. He stood there for a few short breaths, on the spot where he'd normally park his cart, straining his focus on Diego before he stepped back into the night and headed home…

Available now on all Amazon stores

Afterword

I never set out to write a book or become an author. Some people said I was running away when I left London, and to an extent they were right. I was lost. My wife had unexpectedly left me and my job working for a stockbroking company no longer fulfilled me.

I tried travelling around South America and Asia, but that didn't fill my void. Eventually, my travels brought me back to Europe and chance signposts in the form of a Polish barman, a church and a book directed me to the foothills of the Pyrenees. I didn't know it at the time, but I was finally walking the right path. That was in the summer of 2012, in which I walked the Camino Francés, a pilgrimage from Jean Pied de Port to Santiago de Compostela and then onto Finisterre, on Spain's north Atlantic coast. That's thirty-five days of walking, covering 870 kilometres.

It was on my pilgrimage that I regained my self-belief and discovered a voice. The walk and the people I met along the way inspired me to blog about my experience. Those words eventually morphed into a novella (*Candyfloss Guitar*), and then my first novel (*Santiago's Guitar*); ultimately the *Reluctant Pilgrim* series.

In June 2016, I returned to the Camino Francés and walked again from Sarria to Santiago (100 kilometres). Pretty sure of resuming Diego's journey (*Santiago's Guitar*) on that section of the Camino. It was on this route that I unexpectedly discovered I'd soon be taking Diego and myself to Madrid. I also found out that only mad dogs and Englishman visit Madrid in July and August!

In September 2017, I walked the Camino Mozárabe, with my partner, Emma, from Almería on the Mediterranean coast to Granada. Then on my own I walked part of the way to Córdoba. This was some 250 kilometres of walking. Unlike Diego, I only walked the odd day of this Camino in reverse; to see if it was feasible to follow the Camino markers in the wrong direction. Thankfully, for this story it was.

I have attempted to be accurate about the route, geography, villages, towns and cities I name. However, I have applied a writer's license to adapt places for the benefit of the story. The characters are most definitely fictional.

Join My Newsletter

Join Stephen R. Marriott's community to be the first to receive discounts on new book releases, inspiration and other fun things. Most importantly though, building relationships with my readers and the community is the most rewarding thing about being a writer and entrepreneur.

There's no spam, your email is safe and I won't bombard you with emails. You can sign up by visiting my website at:

www.stephenrmarriott.com

See you there!

Enjoyed This Book?
You Can Make A Big Difference

Reviews are the most important way of spreading the word about my books. And readers, like you, are kindly making a big difference by sharing their views.

So if you enjoyed this book, I would be very grateful if you could spare a few moments more by jumping over to the Amazon store your bought the book and leaving a short honest review too.

By sharing your review, you will be bringing my books to the attention of other readers, which will help me continue to build a loyal readership.

Thank you so much.

Acknowledgements

It's been a walk of 350 kilometres, some 68,000 words and numerous drafts and edits. There were those that briefly intersected my path, while others have been there for the entire journey of the book. It would be impossible to thank or even remember everyone that has contributed towards it but what follows is my best attempt to mention the people that have.

Hence in no particular order thank you:

Emma, my loving partner, for always believing in my writing. But especially for being my walking companion and guiding us on those early morning trails, where I was useless until the coffee kicked in. Not forgetting all that tireless proofreading you did.

Bill Traugott for coming on board again, and finding the time in between looking after his kids and farm work. This story may never have seen the light of day if it wasn't for your honest feedback and various forms of editorial guidance.

My amazing Street Team, who were there to give the book a final polish just before its publication.

Calvin Niles and Martin Sealy for your input on the first draft (and showing me there was still much work to be done).

Nate Bunger for putting me up in paradise during the early stages of the writing and Steven Moore for providing the perfect colonial getaway to complete the final stages of the manuscript.

Adam Wells for the translations and adding all those accents I missed.

My Mum, for never doubting and her ubiquitous question every time I visited, "Have you finished the book yet?"

My cover designer, Stuart Bache of Books Covered, for the fantastic design and additional branding service.

Ed Zhao, for the wonderful map illustration. Diego would be proud of it.

Leila Green, my editor, for all your work and patience during our coffee meetings. And of course your team's professional proofreading, typesetting and formatting services.

Bestselling author, Richard Paul Evans, and his team for coming into my life just at the right moment. Your insights and encouragement helped my writing fingers to continue walking.

The staff at Travelling Through bookshop for proving me with mugs of tea during all those hours I spent in your basement café.

The Confraternity of St. James for letting me access your library and maps.

The Almería Jacobea Association for your concern during the freak rain storms.

Paco, for providing two weary pilgrims with a home to rest up in Granada.

All the *hospitaleros*, restaurateurs, bar owners and pilgrims I met along the Camino who befriended and inspired me.

The kind readers and reviewers of *Candyfloss Guitar*, some of whom have gone onto walk their own Caminos. You made me believe there was a second book in me.

About the Author

Stephen R. Marriott is a British author and traveller. His debut book, *Candyfloss Guitar*, book one of the *Reluctant Pilgrim* series, came about because of his desire to walk a road that millions have walked over the centuries. The people and places that intersected his Camino de Santiago pilgrimage inspired his story of a modern-day pilgrim busking his way across Spain, with little more than his dreams and the gift of his father's old guitar.

Before Stephen broke out of the office and went his own way he worked as an investment analyst for a London stockbroking company. When he's not travelling he normally lays his hat in London.

You can also connect with Stephen at:

: www.facebook.com/StephenRCommunity

: @stephenrmarriott

Email: stephen@stephenrmarriott.com

Made in the USA
Lexington, KY
10 January 2019